DISCOVERING LIFE'S TRAILS:
Adventures In Living

Tom Dennard

RAINBOW BOOKS, INC.

DISCOVERING LIFE'S TRAILS: Adventures In Living
by Tom Dennard

Cover Design by Marilyn Ratzlaff
Interior Design by Marilyn Ratzlaff
Cover Photo: Tom Dennard with Lhakpa next to the Dudh Kosi River
Back Cover Photo: Tom Dennard
$14.95
ISBN #0-935834-97-4

Library of Congress Cataloging-in-Publication Data

Dennard, Tom
      Discovering life's trails : adventures in living / by Tom
      Dennard.
      p. cm.
      Includes index.
      ISBN 0-936834-97-4 (acid-free) : $14.95
      1. Dennard, Tom — Journeys. 2. Voyages and travels—1981-
3. Spiritual life. I. Title.
G530.D427 1993   93-2903
910.4—dc20   CIP

All photos by Tom Dennard

ACKNOWLEDGMENTS

Writing for me has only been for the pleasure and purpose of keeping family members informed of some of my travel adventures. After a great deal of coercion and arm-twisting, my cousin, Stephen Doster, attempted to publish some of these stories. Betty Wright of Rainbow Books, Inc., was the ideal person to inspire and nurture me through this arduous process and convince me that it was worthy. I am most grateful to Stephen and Betty for their untiring hours.

Family writers, Annette Peery, Angela Burns, and Pete McCommons critiqued these pieces and constantly reassured me. Also, many thanks to my good friends, Jingle Davis and Jaxon Hice for writing the Foreword. And, of course, thanks to my family, Marie, Susan, Ted, Jeff, and Rufus for their many words and barks of encouragement.

CONTENTS

WHY A HOSTEL?

CHAPTER ONE

CONTENTS
WHY A HOSTEL?

FOREWORD

Many of the people whose hopes and dreams of the future were forged in the idealistic furnace of the sixties somehow lost their fire in the chillier decades that followed. Tom Dennard, who built the Hostel in the Forest, is one notable exception.

Tom's fervor burns just as brightly now as it did in those long-haired hippie days when he marched in peace demonstrations, supported Martin Luther King and the Civil Rights movement, and made the rock festival scene.

A successful attorney and family man, Tom, through the years, has managed to accommodate the realities of everyday life and still follow his dream to one of the most unlikely spots imaginable: an insect-infested jungle in south Glynn County, Georgia, smack in the middle of a rural community whose residents are not generally known for tolerating long-haired hippie lawyer-types. But Tom brought it off.

Those same rednecks who once believed the Hostel housed a bunch of sex-crazed, dope-dealing heathens would probably fight anybody now who had the gall to suggest that Tom and his friends eat collard greens with chopsticks (which, in truth, they probably do).

It is a tribute to Tom's own brand of genius that he built a place beloved by everyone. With creativity, hard labor, and a little help from his friends, who range from hard-core hippies to bank-examiner-types, Tom transformed 90 once-inhospitable acres into a magical place of transcendental peace, ecological balance, and international brotherhood.

Jaxon Hice, who helped erect some of the Hostel's early structures, has vivid memories of those early days when he and the construction crew did yoga headstands every morning before hefting their hammers, to the consternation of visiting building inspectors.

"Tom had a way of bringing the most unexpected individuals together and infecting them with his vision," Jaxon says. "His excitement was contagious. Had Tom not gone into the legal profession, he could have easily been in the ministry. Tom's attentive, open listening makes everyone give their best, their truth. He's genuinely interested in everybody. Maybe that's what the Hostel really is, the Church of Tom."

After the project's contractor suffered a heart attack, Jaxon, now a California contractor, literally got his feet wet in the construction business by taking over the job.

"The domes were surrounded by swamp," remembers Jaxon. "Sometimes after a rain, whole stacks of lumber would float away. Half the vehicles that brought materials got stuck; the other half got lost. The building department thought we were all nuts, but Tom made it happen."

Visitors to the Hostel in the Forest are always curious to know more about the man behind this bucolic paradise.

For the record, Tom Dennard was born in the small town of Pineview, in the heart of Georgia's peanut-farming country near the Ocmulgee River, the same locale where his great-great-grandfather settled in the early 1800s.

Growing up, Tom participated in just about every sport his high school offered. He attended Davidson College in North Carolina, then received his law degree from the University of Georgia.

Tom married Marie Burton; and the couple produced a daughter and two sons during the sixties era when Tom practiced poverty law, establishing the first legal aid office in Brunswick, Georgia. He also served as public defender, representing clients who could not afford to pay for legal assistance.

Tom, who was president of the Glynn County Bar Association and the Young Lawyers of Georgia, was named "Young Man of the Year" in 1971 by the Brunswick Jaycees.

His own extensive travel experience around the globe introduced him to hosteling and prompted his desire to build a hostel of his own. The Hostel in the Forest was the first official youth hostel to open in the Southeastern United States; for years, it was the only hostel in Georgia.

"The Hostel in the Forest is more than a stopover on the road to a new age," Jaxon says. "It is a temporary home for a lot of adventurous travelers seeking their own truth and finding it in the company of Tom Dennard."

What follows is Tom's own account of the building of his Hostel in the Forest. His writing is warm and unaffected, charming and funny and sensitive — a lot, in fact, like Tom himself.

Tom, you kept the faith, and we're proud of you.

Jingle Davis
Jaxon Hice

PART 1

BUILDING THE DOMES

"**W**hy a hostel?" my mother asked. "Will it make money?"

"No, Mama, probably not," I responded wearily.

"Well, then, why on earth would you want to put your money in it?"

That question rang in my ears for many years after the Hostel began. Then, the dividends started rolling in. It had made me rich — not in money, because I've never received one penny from the Hostel — but I hit the jackpot by finding in my life the one thing that provides me with extreme pleasure.

Travel has always been an obsession. From earliest memories of childhood, I was a "map freak." Hours were spent pondering over charts, graphs, plats, and sketches that my father had on every continent. I daydreamed and fantasized many journeys throughout each country, like dog sledding through Alaska, climbing mountains in the Alps, and just seeing many strange and foreign lands. It was not until 1971 that I was able to actually make that first trip abroad. England, France, Switzerland, Germany, Italy, and Spain brought those lifelong illusions into reality.

This first dose of travel was like an aphrodisiac, making my desire insatiable. I craved more and more and more. I wanted to see it *all*. I am one of a very few who even like other people's slide shows of their "summer vacation." And so it came to pass that roaming the world was my obsession, or I should say, "Is my obsession;" and fortunately I've been able to see a lot of it.

Since a wife and three children seemed to have other needs for me, it was necessary to acquire a taste for also traveling vicariously. Talking with adventuresome travelers can be the next best thing to *doing it* yourself.

On a train from London to Paris during that first journey, I learned my new acquaintances were staying in hostels. They had to explain to me what they were! "It is an international organization that provides a clean and safe place to stay overnight."

This sounded as though it might be fun. I decided to sample my first hostel. What a terrific place to meet people and take advantage of a network of travel information! The hostelers told me where to go, where to stay, where not to go, and where not to stay. It also suited my budget; I was adhering to the bible of travel, Frommer's *Europe On $5 A Day.*

Dreams of having my own hostel became more frequent. Unfortunately, I had no money. So how was it possible? My entire life has been a story of luck. Everything has always happened as though I were *Alice In Wonderland.* If I wished really hard for something, it just always seemed to come true.

Searching for land in the Brunswick, Georgia, area was not easy; land owners wanted cash. There was a large tract of 75 acres out on the Waycross highway, about ten miles south of town, but I didn't need that much land for a hostel. Maybe I could buy it, I thought, since the owner was willing to finance the entire purchase price and sell off the highway frontage to help pay for it.

That thought became a reality in February, 1974, and the deal was struck. Annual payments would not be easy, but the law firm had made me a partner; and for the first time in my life, I was able to sock a little cash away.

Where to build the hostel? There were no roads or improvements on the land. The undergrowth was thick with gallberry and briars that made walking practically impossible. Many times I walked the survey lines around the perimeter and made brief efforts to penetrate the interior. Nothing of interest was ever found, except one large oak tree in the center of the property which seemed like a nice spot. But I felt the hostel should be situated toward the rear, especially if the highway frontage had to be sold.

On one of the many hikes along the survey lines, I came upon an animal path that led across the rear boundary of the property onto the adjacent land. It was late afternoon and the sun was about to set.

I should get out of here while there is still light, I thought.

But the trail lured me back into a circle of hardwood trees. Here there was a small clearing where animals, probably deer, slept. A strange peaceful feeling enveloped me. I sat there in a stillness that I had only experienced in a deep meditative state. There was a feeling of calm and tranquillity.

What was this place? Could it have been some spiritual worshipping grounds for Indians? Did animals congregate here for a forest rally?

Many questions ran through my mind as I returned each day. But clearly one answer prevailed and became more apparent. This had to be the spot where the hostel should be constructed.

What the hell? I had just purchased 75 acres of land, about ten times more than I needed: and so I had decided to build a hostel on the adjacent property that I didn't even own. I admit to being crazy, but this was mad.

The tax office was able to provide the name of the owner, a crusty old character who lived down the highway. His name was Mister, or at least that's what everybody called him.

The dirt lane west of the hostel property was named for him; he had been born in the house where the road dead ends.

Mister was a little dubious. My hair was much too long. When I finally told him to name his own price, his curiosity and suspicion mellowed. It was only just one acre that was needed, the place with the circle of hardwoods.

But Mister, who had no formal education, was filled to the brim with wisdom in the ways of the world. He knew a fish when he saw one and was aware that this boy already had the hook set. The only thing left was just the pure enjoyment of reeling him in. "I ain't gonna sell no less than the whole 15 acres, take it or leave it."

My God, I thought, 75 acres is ridiculous, but 90 acres is insane. How will I ever pay for it?

Finally we struck a deal. But Mister's apprehensions have never subsided. To this day, when he sees me, he always asks, "How is that hippie hotel doin'?"

I was now the proud owner of 90 acres of land on U.S. Highway 82 between Brunswick and Waycross,

Georgia. The property was covered with pines and cypress and was very low and swampy. The soil is what the locals call gumbo, which is not a cajun seafood soup, but a black claylike substance. Putting a road on it was not an easy task, though the county public works agreed to clear the roadway, provided the direction was flagged.

With the idea of pushing down as few trees as possible, I set out to pierce the thicket of underbrush. Most of my time was spent crawling on hands and knees. As I crept through the entangled brambles on my belly, I came face to face with a large black snake, staring me down 12 inches from my nose.

The snake's head stood erect. We gazed steadily and intently at each other for a few moments. Finally, the snake turned to the right and slithered away.

In like manner, I turned to the left and scurried away. Thus, the location of the road had no rhyme or reason, except the meanderings along the parts that could be traversed by the determination of a strong-willed spirit and the avoidance of ugly reptiles.

Now a pickup truck became a necessity. I had always wanted a pickup. A client needed to sell his old red Dodge; it seemed perfect, and I purchased it. But invariably it got stuck trying to pass over that cleared avenue of soft gumbo.

It didn't take long for me to grow tired and weary of having to be pulled free from where the pickup had bogged down. That is how I came to know Joe Drawdy, an anomalous old coot, who lived near Mister.

Joe reckoned he could put that road in such shape that I would never get stuck again. There were three cardinal rules for making a dirt road work properly, he told me: "Get the rain water off quick, get it off immediately, and get it off in a hurry."

So, he proceeded to put ditches on both sides of the roadway and fill the bad spots with broken bricks and rubble. You know, he was right. No one, who has driven on the road, has been stuck since, only the many who have run into the ditch.

Toward the latter part of 1974, the REA (Rural Electric Authority) ran an electrical cable down the middle of the road, one meter deep back to the magic circle of hardwoods. Things were beginning to move. But the decision had to be made about the type of building.

One of my contractor clients wanted to construct a concrete block dormitory, but that didn't seem suitable. Someone told me about an old framed, one-room school house in Woodbine, a town about 20 miles to the south. Filled with old desks, probably about 1,000 square feet, it was being sold to the highest bidder and could easily be moved to any location.

I was planning to enter a bid on the school house when my St. Simons Island neighbor, Erv Davis, brought over a brochure on geodesic domes. They were originally designed by Buckminster Fuller. He had lectured on Sea Island the year before. Fuller spoke for three hours, but it had seemed as though it were only 30 minutes. So, I was familiar with domes and knew immediately on seeing the picture that a dome was absolutely perfect in every way.

The big transfer-truck with the pieces of the domes arrived before Christmas, 1974. Like everything I've ever done, I always grossly underestimate the magnitude of any job. The two prefabricated structures seemed small in the brochure and arrangements had been made with a St. Simon's neighbor to stack the triangular frames under her carport. Big joke.

When the truck driver opened up the truck's backdoors, I had assumed only the back end of the cargo would be the dome pieces. The shock set in when I saw material packed like sardines from back to front in the belly of that huge transfer truck. Phones started ringing to friends as I pleaded for help, and thank God, for Bud Paulding and Jay Wetzel; they came to the rescue. We shifted locations to Brady Turner's Storage Yard in Brunswick, and the three of us muscled those heavy frames off that truck all day long.

The building inspector, who was retiring at the end of the year, had never heard of a geodesic dome, and he could find nothing similar to it in his book. Fortunately, one of my senior law partners was the county attorney, and the inspector, out of friendship for him, gave us the go-ahead.

Unanswered letters to the American Youth Hostel Association led me to believe that there would be no assistance from them. They obviously saw no need for a hostel in a Georgia swamp. There was not one in the South and the nearest to Brunswick was in Washington, D.C. However, I remained undaunted; I was determined to proceed. Neither hell nor high water would stop me. We were going to have a hostel whether or not AYH had any interest.

An architect friend, Ed Cheshire, and I agreed that in the center of the circle of trees was the appropriate place. Let the domes rest in that magic spot and make them appear as if they had grown up out of the ground like mushrooms.

A foundation was built by John Cowan. He had constructed our law office building and was as likable a fellow as you would ever meet. Decks were built on the concrete block foundation to accommodate the domes.

We were ready for the big day. But we had to wait for the dome company, Geodesic Structures in New Jersey, to send us the representative to assist in the construction. After a few phone calls to salve my impatience, they agreed to have him there the last weekend in January, 1975.

It had rained for days. Though Joe Drawdy's improved road was passable, there was no way to turn a truck around. All the materials were hauled out on Brady's flatbed truck to the little dirt road, but the driver balked on going any further than the paved highway. I had learned to drive a deuce-and-a-half when I was in the National Guard that didn't even have a back to the seat. So I took over the truck, threw it in reverse, and backed that long flatbed all the way down the narrow one-half-mile trail to the construction site without a bobble. This was repeated each time a delivery truck came out, until I got where I could do it blindfolded.

The big weekend arrived. A guy named John of Geodesic Structures flew in from New Jersey. It had been snowing up there, and the temperature was in the 80's here in Georgia. About ten of my friends had volunteered for the barn raising. My wife, Marie, had prepared refreshments of good food and drinks to keep the workers from getting restless.

At 8:00 a.m. on that January Saturday morning, it all began. The triangular frames had been assembled in the factory. The cedar shake shingles were already attached to the outside and four inches of urethane insulation had been blown into the frames. No nails were used. It was just a matter of bolting the puzzle together.

The atmosphere was one of merriment. Bud

provided continuous music to fit the occasion. People ate, drank, laughed, and worked. It seemed so easy and fun. Frame by frame was handed up to the crew on the deck and passed up to the workers on the scaffolding. It was coming together nicely. The last piece was the only one that took a little doing. We had to pull and tug to make that frame fit into its allotted slot. By five o'clock, the big geodesic dome was completed. It was a time for celebration, which lasted into the night.

All of the crew were "up and at 'em" Sunday morning to erect the smaller dome. Our previous day's experience caused us to go even faster. By noon, it was completed.

We couldn't believe it, two geodesic domes assembled in a day-and-a-half. Our crew had become a team. We were ready to go out and tackle the world. John reluctantly flew back to the Frozen North, but the sheer joy and good vibrations of the occasion lingered on.

The domes were up. Now came the decision on how to arrange the interior. A bathhouse was essential, and we needed decks. Enter Jaxon Hice.

Jaxon had grown up on St. Simons, but had lived for the past several years in his homemade cabin in the California Redwoods. Environmental integrity was his bag, and he had acquired the skills of a darn good carpenter. There was reason for excitement when he agreed to lead the team. Harry Kaufman had been a long-time friend, having graduated from Duke University in North Carolina and Exeter College in England. He was very exacting and had a good pair of hands. Joe Williams was a yoga instructor and a student of Eastern mysticism; he loved carpentry and wanted to work with us. Joe's friend,

Ricky Peek, was a St. Simons surfer but could wield a hammer as good as anybody. What I lacked in skills was overcome by my unbridled enthusiasm.

This was undeniably a great group of guys. We had all survived the sixties intact. The "movement" at this point had taken a more religious bend. It became much more popular to have an Indian Guru than a bag of stash, to be a vegetarian, a devotee of Baba Ram Dass, with a love of nature and a denial of materialism. We were to a man well qualified in all phases. Our hair was at least to our waists, except for Harry's, which reached his ass.

These were high moments. Each sunrise found us performing Hatha Yoga, followed by an hour's meditation. Drugs and alcohol were taboo, only fruits and nuts. We were typical of our generation who were striving to be part of the times. The prevailing demeanor was filled with peace and love, but our occasional appearance in the nearby Brookman community, where the Hostel is located, engendered great fear and loathing.

The word had spread like wildfire that a bunch of hippie freaks were living out there in the woods, and they were certainly up to no good.

When we drove up to Gary's Store for supplies, children ran away and dogs barked. Whereupon the natives jumped into their pickups, locked the doors, and checked the gun racks. On one occasion Gary asked me, "Do you plan to have many rock festivals down there?" To them, that kind of event had every evil connotation imaginable such as drugs, nudism, "free love," and acid rock. It wasn't long before the Sheriff's Department had snooped around behind the trees to observe those weird-looking structures and curious aberrations of nature with the long manes. The phone line was tapped, and one day the common room was bugged when we were all away — to see if this was a prime drug distribution center. Boy, were they ever disappointed.

Each night we sat around discussing what we would do the next day. We never planned more than one day ahead. The diagram for the rooms, loft and bunk room were masterfully designed by Jaxon with the rest of us putting in our two cents. The layout of the office, utility room, and manager's room above left a mighty small two-person kitchen, although it was used for about 12 years before the larger one was built.

Surprisingly, the neighbors heard from the sheriff that there were no illegal activities going on. "Not one of those boys even used any cuss words!" But the community was unconvinced. They conjured up and spread rumors that a nudist colony was in operation back in *them* woods. All snooping voyeurs found us fully clothed. Then, there was the fabrication that a hostel must be a massage parlor, which everyone knew was nothing more than a subterfuge for the most sinful kind of brothel. Unfortunately, none of us had received any massages or sexual favors. Later on, gossip had turned the place into a coven of devil worshipers. This was the last straw.

Realizing that the community needed educating, I prepared a dog-and-pony show complete with slides and brochures. I showed it to every civic club, church group, school gathering, and any other assembly of people interested. Many of the slides were of hostels I had visited in foreign countries. It seemed necessary for them to know that a hostel was *not* hostile.

PART 2

EARLY DAYS OF THE HOSTEL

Our closest neighbors were Cyrus and Wesley who were cousins, although they didn't really like each other. Their skins were black, but that's where the similarity ended. Their families co-existed, but not peacefully, in the only two houses at the end of Mister Road.

Since I was a lawyer, they each would call me about the misdeeds of the other, as if I were a policeman. Both had been there for a long time, and they knew every foot of the Hostel property.

Separately, they told me stories of an old man, who I think was also a cousin, Albert Parlin, who farmed the area back in the 1920s and 1930s. Parlin had planted peanuts, corn, potatoes, and the like. After he died, there was about a 50-year period which permitted the property to go back to nature. The site where the Hostel is located was not farmed, but neither of them knew why.

On the Hostel property near Mister Road were literally hundreds of holes dug to about three feet deep and maybe four feet in diameter. Certainly no animal dug them, unless it was a dinosaur. Cyrus pleaded innocent, but Wesley tattled that Cyrus had used those holes to make charcoal from burned wood. In all of my naïveté, I questioned why he had so many barbecues.

Wesley laughed and said, "Man, don't you know that he uses charcoal to filter his liquor."

I had already discovered the remnants of an old still about 100 feet behind the Hostel. Cyrus never told me about Wesley's involvement, but I suspect that they were probably in it together. Maybe that's why they had a falling out. The only obvious thing was that neither of these old men were too happy about our taking over their secret hiding places.

By the end of June, the domes had been appropriately divided into rooms, a bathhouse built, and decks designed by my architect friend, Ed Cheshire, were securely in place. The new building inspector had been anything but helpful. He had nixed the urethane insulation, claiming that it was highly flammable. We extracted some of it from the frames and put a match to it. Not only did it not explode, but we couldn't even get it to burn.

The building inspector's next pronouncement was that we could not use wood; the code required motels to use only fire retardent material.

"But we are not a motel," we pleaded.

"You charge people to stay there, don't you?" he retorted.

The compromise reached was to pull down all that beautiful red cedar paneling that lined the interior of the common room, and send it down to Jacksonville to be soaked in a salt solution. It was awful when it came back with greenish streaks and powdery white salt. In the sleeping rooms, he made us plaster over the cedar, so that the natural wood effect was completely lost. Finally, all of the county's requirements were satisfied, and a permit was issued for us to open for occupancy on the 4th of July, 1975.

How do you get people to use a hostel? Only $3.00 a night was a bargain in anybody's book. The first response came in from AYH that we could get a charter as the first youth hostel in the South and would be listed in the guidebook for 1976. "But what do we do in the meantime?"

Signs were painted and erected in a few places along the highway. Brochures were prepared and placed at the I-95 Welcome Center. I wrote letters to Scouting groups, schools, and churches to see if they had any desire for a group retreat in the forest. Meanwhile, Harry Kaufman had agreed to stay on as the Hostel's first manager.

One day a boy from Brunswick, Maine, came riding down the trail on his bicycle. It was hard to contain our enthusiasm. Someone had actually found the place by stopping in at the Welcome Center.

The boy received the royal treatment with any choice of the brand new homemade 34 beds he desired, a good meal, lots of advice, and conversation. In fact, he was so enamored with the place, he stayed a second night.

After that, many days and sometimes a week passed without guests. My friend said to me, "You gave a hostel and nobody came." I felt somewhat depressed but hopeful that it would eventually catch on.

We had a meeting one night at my house with Harry, Jaxon, Joe, Ricky, Jingle and Erv, Ed and Selma, Dave, Jonathan, and Marie. The discussion centered around economics.

"Tom, what are you going to do? You've spent tons of money and your return is between $30 and

$50 a month. You gotta do something to get some people to use the Hostel." was the gist of it.

I knew I could probably sell off some of the highway frontage, but I wanted to wait until the last minute. My friends were more worried about me than I was worried about myself. It seemed such a shame to have prepared what to me was a fantastic retreat for nature and no one was taking advantage of it. I had to believe that right would prevail. "All good things come to him who waits," I said.

Those first managers, Harry Kaufman, Parker Mullis, and Bryan Parker, spent a lot of time alone with occasionally one or two hostelers dropping by. On Friday nights, I took my two sons out with their friends, and they had the run of the whole place; for them it was a 90-acre fairyland. Very often some of the locals joined in on Friday nights for a bridge game or scrabble. This gave the lonesome managers something to look forward to. Saturday became a work day for the managers and me. Something always needed to be done.

THE POND

During the summer of our first anniversary, it became painfully apparent that the heat at this time of year was grossly oppressive. We all had grown too accustomed to air-conditioning in our offices and home. Though it was cooler out there under the trees than in Brunswick, it was still hot. We needed a pond to swim in, and it could double as a fish pond. I had visions of sitting on the deck and looking out over an expanse of water. There's something about water for me. I seem to need it around to aid my tranquillity. Like so many of my other fantasies, this too became a reality when we got old Joe Drawdy out there to dig us a fish pond with his bulldozer.

Joe pushed all of the trees up into a large pile that must have been taller than Brunswick's largest building. He then proceeded to burn the pile by throwing old tires underneath it. This resulted in the most gigantic and stupendous fire I had ever seen. Joe didn't seem to be alarmed, but the flames licked the air high above the tallest trees.

The Forestry Department arrived to give us hell for not getting permission to burn, but old Joe remained unruffled. He operated on the theory of doing anything in the world he wanted to do and then asking questions later.

The pile smoldered for days, but there was no question about it, a clearing had been made for a pond. With his backhoe, Joe dug it out about eight feet deep up next to the road and tapered it off to four feet in the rear. What was not taken into consideration, of course, was that the sides would soon cave in and the depth would eventually be about half that.

Our well, which had been dug 750 feet deep, had a natural flow that kept the pond filled with fresh water, and a ditch drained it from the rear. Bass and brim were introduced to allow for eventual fishing, and it doubled as a swimming hole for all of us to escape the heat.

Joe took some of the dirt he had extracted and decided we needed an exit road. "That road you got coming in here is too damn narrow. What if you meet somebody on it?" It seemed to him that it should be a one-way drive with an exit out onto Mister Road and so it was for many, many years.

THE TREE HOUSE

More hostelers began to arrive from countries all over the world. It was gratifying to see how many of them took an interest in the Hostel and its well-being. They volunteered their services and talents to make it the place that it is today.

For example, John McLaughlin was an American who wanted to build a tree house with the extra lumber. This was something we had considered from the beginning but hadn't gotten around to it. John was there — ready, willing and able.

The manager, Lowell, John, my friend Billy, and I put it together in a fairly short time. Can you believe that only 16 nails fastened it to the trees? It turned out to be as much fun to construct as the domes. A rope ladder was the only means of entry and could be pulled up onto the deck. A hatch cover dropped over the opening to provide ultimate privacy.

Poor John accidentally stepped into the hole and found a quick escape route. We thought he had killed himself, and we took him to the hospital emergency room where he was pronounced alive and well. Without skipping a beat, he returned to skillfully finish the job.

Inside the tree house was room only for a double bed. The walls had pine paneling, except the back side, which was all glass so that you could lie in the bed and watch the squirrels playing in the trees. It was romantically designed as the Honeymoon Suite, but everybody wanted to sleep there.

Hostelers had to take turns for the exhilarating experience of swaying in the trees with the wind. When the privilege was awarded to me, I thought my time had come to meet my Maker.

It was a beautiful summer night. But in the wee hours, a storm came over with a nasty little twister. It rained cats and dogs. The wind had the trees bending and swaying. Lightning was popping all around. I had the choice of getting soaked and making a run for it or praying that I was *not* going to come crashing down to the ground. I chose the latter with the prevailing thought that I didn't know of a better way to go than to be entombed in the neatest tree house I had ever seen.

THE TRAILS

Scouting groups from the area came out to sample a little local nature and for weekend outings. A Boy Scout troop chose as its project to cut hiking trails. They came armed with an array of weapons — machetes, bayonets, saws, hatchets, clippers, swing blades, and the like. The assault began soon after breakfast. Those little boys chopped, slashed, hacked, and swung those instruments with deft perception until they found that it was more enjoyable to swing them at each other. The leaders somehow managed to prevent any serious injuries, and by the end of the weekend, they had carved out a passage over one mile long. These trails are still used today where a hiker can see several types of ferns, the insect-eating pitcher plant, and lots of gallberry, cedars, cypress, pines, oak, and gum.

THE CHURCH GROUP

I encouraged groups to use the facilities because it brought in some quick revenue. Many churches used it for their youth and even adult classes. It was sad to see so many of the young people disappointed because there was no television, the rooms had no private baths or carpeting. They felt that this was "roughing it" too much. One Girl Scout group left when they found that it was not air-conditioned.

I always gave these visitors an introductory speech on what hostels were about, how the domes were built, the importance of learning more about nature, and the need to conserve it. Probably most of my words fell on deaf ears; nevertheless, I felt that if only one person was converted, it was worth the while.

We never participated in any of their meetings. They were given the whole bunkroom to do their thing, except for one cold night. A Baptist youth group of about 40 kids wanted to use the common room because it had heat. They were all squeezed into every crook and cranny to hear their guest speaker from Atlanta.

Lowell, Billy, and I retreated to the manager's quarters for a game of hearts in the loft above the office that was open to the common room. They were as quiet as mice which made it difficult for us to pop the tops on our beer cans. All sounds seem to be amplified in those domes. We muzzled the noise under the mattress as the speaker began to condemn the use of alcohol in any form. We tried to control our snickers as the minister castigated the sinners who danced and played cards. By this time, we were holding our hands over our mouths and rolling on the floor. Then, he told them to beware of the worst sin of all — masturbation. At this, Lowell laughed out loud, which was very disconcerting to the preacher. Fortunately, in a round house there is no way to discern the origin of the sound, so he thought it was one of the students.

We were trapped up there for at least two hours. There was no way to get down through the mass of bodies. We never let that situation happen again.

SEGER'S ROADIES

It was not often that we had rock concerts locally, but the word spread like wildfire that Bob Seger was going to play at the Aquarama on Jekyll Island. A few days before the big event, the stage crew booked the Hostel. I'm not sure how they found out about it, but they began arriving in various odd vehicles. It was night when the truck containing all of the lighting equipment found its way to that little dirt road that leads to the Hostel.

When the large paneled truck tried to make the turn on that first hairpin curve, it ran into the ditch and turned over on its side. The woman driving was in a state of shock. She was running up and down, screaming about how many hundreds of thousands of dollars worth of lights were on that truck.

We tried to calm her down, then called a wrecker. They looked at the truck and insisted that it would take two wreckers. So, one came in from the exit road; and they got on both ends of the truck and pulled it out. Throughout the entire ordeal, the woman was cursing loudly at everyone in a wild and irrational manner. Fortunately, all of the equipment was intact and when the truck was free, she calmed down somewhat. But paying for two wreckers was not in her budget.

Any time you have a group of roadies from a rock band, there's bound to be at least one oddball in the crowd. One fellow looked as mean as a snake; he never said a word to anybody. He nervously walked around with this scowl on his face. The others seemed afraid of him, especially the pretty girl who was with him. I didn't know if she was his wife or girlfriend, but he apparently had her under his thumb.

One night we all sat around the common room having a few beers and playing darts. It came down to a play-off between the girlfriend of the evil man and me. As we threw the darts and laughed, he jumped up, grabbed her, and hauled her out the door. I suppose he'd decided she was having too much fun with another man. No one thought too much about it; and we finished off the evening with dance music.

That night I slept in the manager's room over the office. Ever since I can remember I have slept in the nude, whether it is hot or cold. But this was a warm summer night, so I had no covers. At some point, I was startled out of a dead sleep to find the nude body of that girl lying beside me.

The shock sent waves of adrenalin rushing through my body. "What are you doing here?" I sat up, covering my body with the sheet.

"I'm afraid he's going to kill me," was her reply.

"My God, I have a wife and three children. I don't want him to kill me, too." At this point the front door slammed. Heavy footsteps marched around and then out the door with another slam.

"He will kill us if he finds us here!" She was shaking.

"But nothing has happened between us!"

"He will never believe it," she lamented.

"Look, you gotta get out of here now." I spoke in a panic.

"But, I'm afraid."

"Yeah, so am I."

She finally left, much to my happiness. My heart was beating at an accelerated rate. I secured the hatch cover down tightly so no other intruders could come up to my private sleeping quarters.

All of the stage crew left early the next morning and I never knew what happened to her. My fear hung around for days. The only thing I knew for certain was that I never wanted to die at the end of the gun of a jealous lover.

GROUP USE

There is no telling how many times over the years, we had to call a wrecker to pull some car, truck, or bus out of the ditch. We kept the number of a wrecker service prominently displayed over the telephone.

One weekend, a high school group from some town in North Georgia was booked in. There were 62 kids who arrived, and I had borrowed tents from everyone I knew. It really looked like tent city all around the pond.

That Friday evening all of them were wildly chasing each other all over the place. One of them jumped from the deck on top of the outside faucet next to the steps leading to the old tree house and broke the whole pipe off. Water was gushing out about ten feet. At the same time, a young man came walking up to tell me that his bus was in the ditch.

"What bus?" I yelled as I put my hand over the gushing water pipe.

"The University of Georgia bus," was his answer.

"What do you mean?" I ignored the water and ran to look for the manager. It seems he had mistakenly booked in two groups for the same weekend.

He and I hurried down the road to see the headlights of a Greyhound bus shining from the ditch on that famous first curve. This nice man, Robert Saveland, an Environmental Science Professor at the University of Georgia, had brought 25 students who were all excited about getting to sleep in their first hostel.

I've always felt that I could do the impossible, but this may have been my greatest test. The Hostel has 34 beds and a loft in the bunk room where maybe ten people can throw a sleeping bag. 62 plus 25 makes 87. What would we do with all of these people?

The wrecker company was always happy to receive a call even though it was past midnight. This situation also required a wrecker on each end to remove that massive hunk of metal out of Joe Drawdy's deep ditch. As I watched the awesome display of the Greyhound bus being lifted from the ground, thoughts were racing through my mind: How are you going to juggle this one, Tom, old boy?

The high school kids were a really nice group with understanding leaders. We got them to double up in the tents to provide an empty bunkroom for the tired university students. Mind you, there was no water, because we had to turn off the main valve to prevent the creation of a lake underneath the bathhouse. What a dilemma.

The good Lord fed the multitudes with two fishes and a loaf of bread. That night *He* endowed me with similar powers. We repaired the water early the next morning and miraculously made it through the weekend with no more unfortunate events. The manager and I vowed never to allow this to happen again. Groups provided us with a much-needed infusion of cash, but they took a toll on the Hostel, and 87 was beyond the ridiculous to the sublime.

THE PICKUP TRUCK

The old pickup was rusting badly. Above the windshield, the metal had been completely eaten away. On a cold day, towels were stuffed in the gapping hole to prevent frost bite. The paint was flaking and peeling. It was not exactly a beauty on wheels when it rolled up to the bus station to pick up the curious and somewhat reluctant hostelers. The tailgate would not stay closed. Sometimes it would just fall open and scare the hell out of the guests sitting in the back.

One day I drove into town to pick up a lawn-mower from the rental shop to mow the hiking trails. It was a large mower with two bicycle wheels. At that time, I-95 was completed only to Exit #7, so traffic poured off into the two-lane road where it followed Highway 303 to a truck stop and then reunited with I-95 south. It was practically impossible to enter the highway where there was no stop light. But I sat there for what seemed like hours, waiting for a break in the bumper-to-bumper traffic.

The ticking of the rental meter for the lawn-mower gave rise to my impatience. Suddenly I spot-ted a small space between the line of cars. I gunned the accelerator and sped into the congestion, entirely forgetting about the mower and the temperamental tailgate. I turned around in time to see the lawnmower sailing unimpeded down the road amidst curious onlookers. It seemed as though it had been shot out of a cannon, landed upright, and was racing away from me at a fast rate of speed. How do you catch a runaway lawnmower? I don't know, but I did it. Very shortly thereafter we traded the old red pickup for a dandy little yellow Ford — with a good tailgate.

THE MIDNIGHT INTRUDERS

On a warm Saturday night, we had stayed up past midnight playing scrabble. It always amazed me how people from non-English-speaking countries could out-spell us in our own language. As the last one to bed, I turned off all lights so that only the moon slightly illuminated the domes underneath the trees. No sounds could be heard, except the crickets and the tree frogs repeating their rain mantras. I closed the door to Room #2 and was asleep within 30 seconds. At some point the sound of heavy footsteps woke me, and the door to my room was flung open.

"Hey, anybody in there?"

Although it was dark, I could make out the massive frame of a black man, dripping wet, and filling the doorway. He was mumbling something about me coming out there. I could see the headlights of an automobile shining directly toward the Hostel.

The man was obviously drunk. He could hardly walk. But I slipped on my pants and walked with him out onto the grounds.

The car appeared to be floating on the pond. But how could it sit on top of the water?

His female companion was standing out there, scared to death. "Please, mister, come get us out of this place," she begged.

I couldn't help but laugh. Obviously, being equally intoxicated, she had driven their car down the lonely little dirt road, looking for a good parking place. When she saw the buildings, she decided to turn around. But she had backed out onto the small dock that we used for diving, the one that extended into the pond. This meant the passenger's side of the car was suspended in the air over eight feet of water.

When her boy friend opened the door to get out, you can imagine what happened. It was almost enough to sober him up, but not quite.

The girl friend continued to plead, "Please, mister, just get us out of here. I'll pay you any amount of money you want. Just please get out of this place!"

I went for the pickup and tow chain that we used to get the easy ones out of the ditch. Without too much difficulty, the car came right off the dock. I jumped inside to back it out and, boy, did it reek of alcohol! Then, I turned the car around and drove it a few feet down the road to get them straightened out.

"Praise the Lord, I thank you, Lord. I do thank you. We won't never come back here again," the girl friend bellowed. "I just thank you so much. Hey, Joe, give that boy a quarter."

MULLET SMOKING

One of my favorite pastimes in the summer is seining. I have a net that's 100 feet long with a pole on each end. We get all of the hostelers and go to the beach in front of my house. One or two people take each pole and pull it around in the ocean. We have caught an incredible number of fish that way. Normally we net mullet, croakers, spots, trout, spanish mackerel, flounder, sheephead, drum, and always a few crabs and stingrays. This makes for a nice community meal at the Hostel. Usually the fish are cooked over a barbecue with a sauce or marinade for basting. All of the hostelers really enjoy this, since it is something that they have never done before.

We had built a mullet smoker, which was nothing more than a plywood cabinet about the size of a refrigerator with racks every few inches to place the fish. Ours would hold 130 good sized mullet, and many times we would have parties and eat smoked mullet. Those things are delicious, especially with a cold beer. A lot of friends from Brunswick and St. Simons would come out to help us eat them. The music was brought outside and people would dance; and before the night was over everyone got thrown into the pond.

My friend, Rick Shelnutt, and I were pulling the seine one Sunday afternoon. There were other people out there doing the same, and they were all pulling in empty nets. We decided to move further down and give it another try. All of a sudden we hit a school of mullet. They were hitting the net like crazy. We pulled it in, knowing that we had scored a big one. There were 136 mullet in that net.

All of the other people who had been skunked looked at us in amazement. It was like a scene from the Bible. Fish were jumping everywhere. Needless to say, this made a very fine party at the Hostel.

RATTLESNAKE SUPPERS

Rick, who works on Sea Island, talked to the man who is in charge of killing snakes on the resort island. "Some of the rattlesnakes lie in the sand dunes," he said. "You can only see their eyes because they're buried in the sand, waiting for a mouse, frog, or bird. It's not a good idea to step on them." He had killed three large rattlers about as big around as your arm and maybe five feet long. So, it seemed obvious to us that we should have a rattlesnake supper at the Hostel.

Actually, the meat is pretty tasty. The texture is like chicken, but it doesn't have quite the same flavor. But a rattlesnake supper became routine every time this guy gave us enough snakes. We always had to have the cookout at the Hostel, because Marie would not let me bring even dead rattlesnakes in our house. She even threw the pans away that I cooked them in.

We tried broiling it, putting it on the barbecue grill, baking it with a white wine sauce, but our favorite way was frying up small pieces of it like Kentucky Fried Chicken. Anyway, late one afternoon, the Hostel manager had brought in three huge rattlesnakes that had not been skinned, but their heads had been cut off. He was busy so he just threw them down on the floor next to the sign-in register.

Shortly, three French boys came walking in with their backpacks. When they saw the snakes, two of them ran out of the door. The other one, scared out of his wits, said, "What eez that?"

The manager very casually said, "Oh, that's just tonight's supper."

THE DARKEST DAY

In 1979, Roger Bowen, the Australian blond bomber, became the Hostel manager. His good looks and flowing curls made all the girls nervous. We kidded him a lot about a beautiful Swedish girl who stayed for a few days.

It was Labor Day, the first Monday in September, and we had caught loads of mullet. There were more than enough for a big party. Hurricane David was threatening but had less than 100 mph winds. That night we had a great party. A lot of new hostelers had arrived. Jacques and Dominique were best friends from a suburb outside Paris. They had been traveling all over America. Murray, an English lad, was headed to Jamaica but got off the bus to avoid the hurricane. There were the usual number of Germans, a couple of Americans, Wallace Harrell being one of them. During the party, a hitchhiking French boy named Marc arrived to help us devour some smoked mullet and a few beers. It was the first time we had ever had a hurricane party at the Hostel, but we never needed much excuse to have some fun.

Due to the hurricane, Marie and the kids stayed with me at the Hostel, since our house was right on the beach. The wind blew hard and one of the trees fell out in front of the domes. Fortunately, no damage was done.

The next morning things seemed to have quietened considerably. The eye of the storm had passed by out at sea during the night. We cleaned up limbs and debris. The fallen tree would need a chain saw, so we saved it until later.

Marie and I packed up all our gear to head on back home. Roger said that some of the hostelers wanted to go over to the beach in front of my house and take a swim in the surf. The rough seas would be fun compared to its usual gentle state.

"Just be careful!" I said as we drove away.

In front of our home, a sandbar was separated from our beach by a channel. Many times we swam over to it and walked around, chasing sea gulls, pelicans, and the other water birds. When the tide came in, the channel was more difficult to swim since the current pulled to the north into Gould's Inlet.

From my bedroom window that day, I saw eight people playing on the sandbar. With my binoculars, I could see Roger, Murray, Wallace, a German girl, an American boy with one arm, and the three French boys. Because of the tail end of the hurricane, the waters were really rough and choppy. The wind was bringing the tide in unusually fast. My phone rang. It was Robin Skelton, my neighbor.

"Are these people from your Hostel out there in that water?"

I told her they were.

"Do you think they're safe?"

"They're all good swimmers, but I'll go out and check on them."

By that time, eight heads were bobbing in the waves about 200 yards off shore. The channel was pulling them to the north. Those of us who are accustomed to this condition know that you don't panic; you just let the current take you into the river where you can easily swim to shore. But they didn't know that and were fighting to swim against that swift pull of the water.

The wind and waves were so noisy, they couldn't hear my screams to them. It was obvious they were in trouble.

I ran out into that raging giant of nature. I felt so helpless. Who do you go to first?

Over the white caps I could see that they had begun to touch the bottom. But the shock hit me when I saw Roger carrying the lifeless body of Dominique, a good-looking, dark-haired French boy.

Neighbors had seen what was happening and had called the Coast Guard. We pulled his body up into the sand and started giving him artificial respiration. Sea water was gushing out of his nose and mouth and very soon he began to cough. We were crying for joy as the Coast Guard took him off to the hospital emergency room.

When we started counting heads, Jacques and Marc could not be found. We all ran up and down the beach yelling and screaming their names. The German girl said she saw Marc go down in the water, and she didn't know if he ever came up. In my whole life, I had never felt so much panic and fear.

Some of us went out into the water, but there was no sign of them. We were terrified. But what could we do?

The Coast Guard had organized a search party that hunted the dark waters all night. The police came to my house to get statements. Roger was devastated. He, as manager, felt so guilty. Murray was helpful in calming fears and took the German girl, the American boy, and Wallace back to the Hostel. Roger and Dominique were in no condition to go anywhere.

After a toddy as a sedative, the two boys slept

right next to Marie and me. It was much too frighten-
ing to be alone. We all needed each other for comfort.

Over the years of living on the beach, I have
pulled at least six drowning people out of the water.
As a former lifeguard on the beach, I was trained in
life-saving. Why couldn't I have saved those other
two French boys? Their drowned bodies washed up
on the beach the next day. Going to the morgue to
identify their bodies was the worst day of my life and
the saddest day ever in the history of the Hostel.

SATURDAY BREAKFASTS

Murray, who had felt a sense of bonding because of the catastrophe, agreed to stay on as an assistant manager with Roger. His sense of urgency to get to Jamaica was waning, and the two of them had an unforgettable impact on the Hostel. They were the life of every party, fun to be around, and good managers. That particular era sticks in my mind as being one of my favorite times at the Hostel.

Always on Friday nights, I would stay at the Hostel. On Saturday mornings it seemed to me that all of those foreigners needed to be introduced to grits cooked Southern style. It was not optional, they had to eat the grits or at least try them. Grits are not just a food in the South, but kind of a sacrament. I'm not really even sure if Southerners like grits. But because Yankees have derided us over the years about them, we would eat them even if it killed us. Usually, Gary's homemade sausage, streak of lean bacon, scrambled eggs with cheese, toast and jam, tea and coffee would be spread out on the table. We always ate on the deck, if the weather permitted. Within a couple of years when Harvard University's book *Let's Go America* was published, the article on Georgia went something like this:

"On the Coast of Georgia you should stop in at the Hostel in the Forest in Brunswick. The town is an industrial cesspool that is not worth seeing, but you must stop there long enough to telephone the Hostel to get directions. Only God himself could find that place. Try to be there on Saturday morning when Tom, the owner, prepares his famous Southern breakfast. They eat those God-awful things called grits. What is not eaten is used to patch the roof."

THE MOUNTAINMAN OF B.C.

The amount of talented and unusual people who continue to flock to the Hostel never ceases to amaze me. When a plumber is needed, miraculously some plumber from Australia will appear who is ready, willing, and able to lend a hand. This goes for electricians, carpenters, and cabinet-makers. We even get doctors, lawyers, priests, and judges but thus far have not had any use for their talents.

One character who I remember was an old man at least in his seventies. He had long gray hair and a goatee.

Unquestionably a man of few words, he lived in a log cabin up in the mountains of British Columbia that he had built himself. There's no telling how long he had lived there alone before he decided to do a little traveling. Thumbing was his normal means of transportation and he thought nothing of walking the ten miles into Brunswick and back.

There was always a big pot of soup on the stove which provided his only means of nourishment. The ingredients came from various kinds of plants foraged from the woods, occasionally spiked with a fish from the pond. A work exchange was arranged to pay for his overnights. To my knowledge, in the two weeks at the Hostel, he never spent one penny. An amazing creature, he was totally un-American.

At the time our eating table was a bit creaky. He found some old two-by-fours stored underneath the bathhouse. With nothing but a handsaw, some nails, and a hammer, he created the most sturdy table you would ever want, certainly better than you could buy. We are still using it today, and it will probably be there as long as the Hostel lasts. As a matter of fact, three Australian girls danced on it one crazy night, and that table never even wobbled.

WILLIE AND LOUISE

Willie and Louise are our closest neighbors. They live up on the highway and spend each day sitting on their porch waving to each car that passes by.

Willie is a large man. His hand is as big as my thigh, and his voice is louder than if it were amplified. When he throws that large black hand up to wave to all the cars and yells, "Hey, now?" it can be heard for miles.

Louise is a short, stout lady who laughs all of the time in a high shrill voice.

Anytime I am feeling down and want to get better, a visit to Willie and Louise is just what the doctor ordered. They always keep me laughing and I leave with a smile on my face.

It was traditional on Saturday afternoons for them to have a bottle of gin and a large bowl of boiled eggs for all of their guests to partake. They would sit out under the shade of the old chinaberry tree and receive friends all day long. Their yard full of chickens provided plenty of eggs that were appropriately washed down with a swig from the bottle. Much laughter and merriment took place, and it always made me feel good after a visit with them.

They have nothing materially, that is, but are so filled with good spirit and love. Their only income is a Social Security check. Neither of them can read nor write, but I noticed the mobile library would stop by their house. Come to find out, the only member of the family who could read was their blind daughter who read books to them in braille. It certainly makes one reassess the so-called American way of life.

Many of the hostelers go over and sit on their porch to learn for themselves what I'm talking about. Those two get more cards and letters from foreign countries than anyone I know. Every manager, when their time at the hostel has finished, goes to bid them good-bye and leaves crying like a baby.

If I was told to search for the happiest person in the county, I wouldn't start on Sea Island where the rich millionaires live. I would go directly out the Waycross Highway to the Brookman community and stop in at the home of Willie and Louise.

THE PAKISTANIS

Murray was the manager who came to the Hostel for a night and wound up staying for two years. He met a local girl who had brought out a group of Girl Scouts for a weekend; and it was love at first sight. They married and still live in the area with their two sons.

While Murray was managing the Hostel, he received a call one night from the captain of a merchant ship docked in Savannah. Captain Looney was from Scotland and had grown up hosteling in the British Isles. He wanted to bring his 35 crewmen so they could experience a hostel for a weekend. In fact, Captain Looney had already arranged for his crew to take a Greyhound bus from Savannah to Brunswick.

"How far is the Hostel from the bus station?" he asked.

"Oh, about ten miles," Murray answered. "But we can get a truck and a car, and shuttle you out here."

"That's not a problem," Captain Looney said sternly. "I'll just march them out there."

When Murray told me about this, I decided to meet the bus in Brunswick that Friday evening and use all of my persuasive abilities to get the bus driver to drop them off at the I-95 intersection, only two miles from the Hostel. The bus driver wasn't the least bit reluctant; he was very eager to get rid of them. This was my first knowledge that the entire crew was from Pakistan. Murray drove the old hostel pickup down to the truckstop to wait for them.

The little, red-haired captain jumped off the bus followed by 35 dark-skinned and diminutive Pakistanis. Nothing would do but that he had to march them to the Hostel. We begged them to use the pickup and my station wagon, but no.

What a sight it was seeing this old sea captain calling cadence for his troops as they marched down the highway past Gary's Store toward the Hostel at ten o'clock at night. All passing cars almost ran off the road staring at them. This confirmed all of the neighbors' suspicions that we were crazy as hell.

Shortly after arrival, the captain bedded down the troops and joined Murray and me by the old buckstove in the common room. He liked his Scotch and pulled out a bottle as he settled into the stuffed chair for an evening of old war stories.

All of the Pakistanis were Moslems, and they never failed to regularly render their prayers. They wanted to have turkey for their Saturday night supper. I told them that I would drive some of them to the Winn-Dixie grocery store, but they explained that they could not eat the meat if it were not slaughtered according to Islamic traditions. They reckoned that it was necessary to have a live turkey, since there were no Moslem markets in Brunswick.

I knew a lady on Blythe Island who raised all kinds of fowl, and, sure enough, she had turkeys. They went out to her place and brought three squawking turkeys back to the Hostel.

After fetching the Hostel's sharpest knife, they all congregated out by the pond with their Koran in hand. But they seemed befuddled.

One of them came running back into the common room where we were sitting. "Mister! Mister

Murray! Can you please tell us directions of Mecca?"

Without missing a beat, Murray instantaneously responded, "Oh, it's over there on the other side of Gary's Store." He pointed in that direction as if he really knew.

We looked at each other in disbelief but later found out that it was necessary to aim the poor turkey's head toward Mecca.

Two of them held the handle of the knife and swayed back and forth to the chants of all their surrounding brethren. Our horrified feathered friend was making dreadful noises. The panic-stricken bird died of fright, I firmly believe, before the blade ever pierced the jugular veins.

At this very moment, Willie and Louise came walking up for a visit. Willie's eyes were larger than saucers. "My God! What's goin' on out there?" he said.

Our neighbors around the Hostel have never quite understood what happens there, but this was a little too weird. Willie found little comfort in the fact that their skin was dark like his.

Louise was holding on to him for dear life when these 35 Pakistanis ran past them holding the headless bodies of three turkeys with blood pouring profusely from their necks.

One of the boys followed behind ceremoniously carrying the severed heads.

Willie, always known for being friendly, spoke to one of them, "Hey, Bro, what's happenin', man?"

The boy turned toward him and with a perfect English accent acknowledged his elder. "I beg your pardon, sir?"

Willie was taken aback. He didn't speak like any black man he had ever heard.

It seems that it is the custom in Pakistan if two

boys are friends that they always hold hands when they walk. Several couples began strolling about with hands clasped together as if they were lovers. Willie and Louise could take no more of this ominous crowd of folks, so they scurried on back down the road.

That evening our bellies were filled with the meat of those birds that died in such a horrific manner. It was then time for the entertainment. They sang light and lively songs of their days and nights at sea. They went on to sing patriotically about their beloved country and all of its natural beauty. The roof was raised in joyful song. Before they departed, they had completely endeared themselves to us. We couldn't help but feel a lump in our throats when Captain Looney called them for formation on Sunday morning, and we watched them parade down the road toward the bus station as he sounded cadence loud and clear.

THE CHOOKS

Murray had a notion that the hostelers should have fresh eggs for breakfast so we needed to get us some chickens, or "chooks" as the Australians call them. He went down to talk with old Joe Drawdy. Joe consented to give us a pair of chickens provided that we would come back to his place that night to catch them.

This is accomplished by taking a board and holding it up next to the limb where they are roosting. While someone shines a flashlight in the dumb chickens' eyes, they can be nudged off their perch and onto the end of the board. Then you let it down slowly, until they can be grabbed and thrown into a bag. Now you know how to steal a chicken.

Chickens are, without a doubt, the stupidest creatures in the world. When a 'possum creeps up to invade their sleeping quarters, they do nothing to defend themselves except squawk in hopes that their master comes out and shoots the 'possum. Well, anyway, we bagged a big colorful rooster and a reddish brown hen. I'm not even going to tell you what Joe called them, but they were named Leroy and Liza.

Murray had constructed a very nice hen house with a fenced-in yard, but they only wanted to sleep in the trees. It took a lot of feedings in their newly designed space to get them trained to use it. Leroy was a "cocky" old bird who strutted around the Hostel grounds filled with a generous portion of male ego. He was a little off on heralding the dawn, however, because he did most of his crowing around midnight. Maybe this was his attempt to get the hostelers to go to bed.

As time went by, Leroy became depressed. In talking with other chicken owners like Cyrus and Massey, we learned that, like a lot of males, it takes more than one female to keep them happy. Cyrus reckoned that one cock can service about 12 hens. So Leroy was delighted when Murray drove up with the pickup filled with clucking females. He was never depressed again and was the king pin of the Hostel yard. His harem seemed to be happy, and they produced loads of eggs for the hungry hostelers.

A lot can be learned by observing chickens. There is more than just a small comparison between them and us. They have their "pecking order" where certain hens try to rule the roost. Some get picked on, or should I say, pecked on, which is not at all unlike the secretarial pool at our office.

Leroy also had a similar way about him. He would go just beyond the edge of the yard and start scratching around while making a very distinct clucking sound. A hen would come running and bend over to taste the morsels that he had uncovered. This was his signal to give them a "roll in the sack." I have an old friend who is no different. Only, he has to take his date out to a fine dinner with a good bottle of wine.

One Saturday afternoon a van pulled up in front of the dome. A tall, slender man asked for Tom. After identifying myself, he said that he heard we had chickens. That fact was most obvious because not only were they abundantly in evidence, but it was quite important that one should watch where he or she stepped. He had a most formal Oxonian accent;

obviously he wasn't from the Brookman community. Over a cup of tea, I learned that he was from London and had been living on one of the islands writing a book.

"Have you published?" I inquired.

"Well, yes, I have," he acknowledged.

"Was it a novel?" I asked.

"No, it was the *American Heritage Dictionary*," he said.

That night when I got home, I opened my large hardback dictionary and, sure enough, the first page gave credit to Peter Davies, my afternoon guest, as the editor.

Well, it seems that he had bought a newly hatched chick from a farmer as a pet. It had grown into a pretty large white hen. Now that he had finished his work, he was going back to New York and needed a good home for her. With apologies, he admitted that she had never seen another chicken and really didn't care to stay out in the yard. She had become imprinted and was totally unaware of what her true nature was.

Often when he would leave his cabin, she would chase his jeep down the road as far as she could run. They obviously had quite a thing for each other, and it was with deep emotion and sadness that he asked us to please give her a home.

We agreed that we would take good care of her as he made his tearful farewell. He implored us to write him and tell him of her well-being. We agreed.

We named her Hen. Hen had absolutely nothing to do with any of the other chickens and deliberately stayed as far away from them as possible. She refused to sleep in the henhouse and preferred a myrtle tree out by the pond. We thought her to be quite aloof, smug, and down right arrogant. Having been raised around the writing of a dictionary had apparently rubbed off on her, and frankly, she was an effete snob. None of our yardbirds would even look at her, much less speak to her.

One day we noticed old Leroy edging up over into Hen's territory. He tried his scratching and clucking routine to no avail. He was perplexed but remained undaunted. As he sidled up to her, she ran away. He followed her with a fixed determination. He had almost used up his whole bag of tricks, but suddenly one of them struck home. She was his.

From that moment on Hen was a hen. Leroy had brought meaning and purpose into her life. No longer was she a self-centered snob. She went into the chicken house that night and pecked her way up the ladder of chicken hierarchy. Although she never replaced Liza as Leroy's true love, she became one of his most favorite of all. She dutifully laid an egg each day, but somehow her need for human companionship had not diminished.

Many times she had the audacity to stroll into the common room and nest on the sofa with hostelers sitting all around. Without any qualms or shame, she deposited her egg right there in front of everybody, exhibiting a total absence of inhibitions.

One morning our prissy hen sauntered into the room where an Australian girl was fast asleep. The hot night had forced her to crack the door to the room to allow some incoming air. Hen had the gall to jump up on top of the girl's sleeping bag and lay an egg. Her cackling woke the girl, who came marching into the common room holding the egg with the pronouncement, "I've heard of breakfast in bed, but this is ridiculous."

In a few years, I had the big idea to replace the aging brood of hens with some new young biddies. They were all hybrid Rhode Island Reds that grew unusually fast. Though they were all supposedly females, two of them turned out to be roosters. They became enormous, at least twice as large as Leroy. An uneasiness prevailed in the chicken yard so we penned them up. One day there was a *coup d'état*. Those two young teenagers beat the crap out of poor old Leroy — left him for dead.

I picked up his almost lifeless body. One of his eyes was hanging out. The humane thing to have done would be to take him out of his misery. But I didn't have the heart.

Leroy laid around by the pond for days. It hurt to see this once proud king of the coop in such a pitiful condition. After a time, he took a turn for the better. He sort of perked up a little and began to eat some cracked corn. It was good to see him back on his feet again.

A few days later, I was in the midst of a prolonged real estate closing in my office and was interrupted by an emergency call from the manager. "Did you know that Leroy somehow got back into that chicken pen and killed both of those roosters deader than hell?"

I rejoiced. The king had returned to rule supreme for many years thereafter.

THE SWIMMING HOLE

It was surprising to me that hostelers were arriving with plans to spend one night but wound up staying three or four nights or more. I had assumed that unless they were entertained each day by going to the Okefenokee Swamp, Cumberland Island, the beach, or wherever, then they would move on. It amazed me that there were actually a lot of people like me who found contentment by just sitting in the woods and doing nothing. This can easily be accomplished, except in July and August, the most hateful time of the year. The temperature and the humidity both hover around the high 90s. This makes for a low energy level, and movement only occurs when absolutely necessary.

The fish pond was no longer good for swimming; a close friend, Bruce Faircloth, had planted anacharis in it for his aquarium, and it spread like wild fire all over the pond. It was and still is referred to as the "Bruce weed," but the fish and ducks love it. So what we really needed was a nice cool water swimming hole.

I wanted to somehow duplicate Pappy Jack, a large spring about the size of the hostel geodesic dome, near Pineview, Georgia, the town where I grew up. As kids, we would hitch, bike, or walk the three miles to this spot where ice cold water bubbled out of the ground. The water was deep, and my cousins taught me to swim at age five by throwing me into the middle of it and telling me to swim or drown. Only males frequented the place, since it was unheard of to wear a swim suit.

Joe Drawdy, who claimed to be able to do anything, said he could dig a large enough hole but knew that the sides would cave in the same way the fish pond did. We talked about a retaining wall. "What if we built a wooden fence inside it? Would that work?"

Old Joe was willing to try anything. It didn't matter to him. So he brought his backhoe down and dug a pretty good sized pit about ten feet deep.

A friend, who worked at the Georgia Power Company, gave me a bunch of wooden creosoted poles that they had replaced with their new ugly metal ones. Joe had a saw mill that he used to cut them into thick boards. Some of the poles were used as posts. After sharpening one end, he drove them into the ground with the bucket of the backhoe while some of us stood in the mud holding them in place. All the time we prayed that the bucket wouldn't miss the top of the pole and hit us on the head. We then nailed the boards onto the poles and hoped the pressure of the water would equal the pressure of the dirt outside the wall. Plastic was rolled over the bottom and held down by roofing tiles from the house that was demolished next to mine. Our 750-foot-deep well had a good strong natural flow. The retaining wall worked for about ten years until one side finally gave way and caved in.

There were many good times in that old swimming hole. In the late 1970s, when it was constructed, everyone, even the English, skinny-dipped on hot summer nights. I remember one terribly scorching August day, three Australian girls came walking up the path loaded with heavy backpacks. When they saw cold fresh water flowing into our homemade pool, they dropped their packs and clothes and ran over for a refreshing dip. The Aussies always seem to be the most uninhibited.

The 1980s generation seemed different from the 60s crowd. They felt more comfortable being modestly clothed when they used the new cement-block pool built by Mark, the Irishman, in 1987. Except for one hot Saturday afternoon.

Bruce, Ted, and I were cooling off our nude bodies, since no one else was around. With all of our splashing and horseplay, we didn't hear the 15 Girl Scouts and their two adult leaders approaching. When they ran up beside the pool, it was too late to escape. The older women thought this was no place for their girls and hurriedly led them away, never to return.

As a matter of fact, most of the males quit skinny-dipping when a prankish hosteler caught one of the large-mouthed bass from the fish pond and threw it in the swimming hole. I had once seen an underwater video in which a bass had eaten a three-foot water snake. Even though none of the males I noticed seemed to have any worries, it still put a damper on skinny-dipping.

THE PSYCHIC

In 1980, Al Brown, an old friend, phoned me to let me know that a world-renowned psychic was in the area. He had had a session with her, and she told him some pretty incredible things about himself. He and I had many times talked about our desire to have a reading from a good soothsayer; and this psychic had been employed by the Atlanta Police Department to try to uncover the murderer of the many black children.

I arranged to meet her on Jekyll Island at a motel where she was staying. I hadn't given her my name. If she was a fake, she might call some people in the area to find out something about me. When I met her in the lobby, there was an immediate disappointment. She looked so normal . . .

We decided to try to find a spot on the beach where we could be alone. We drove in my car to a deserted parking lot next to a sea wall, where no one was around to disturb us. The wind and fog made it seem surrealistic. I was nervous.

The psychic only asked my birthdate and the time of birth as nearly as I knew it. I thought she was going to work out some kind of astrological chart. I had already had that done and was not at all interested in another one. They are always so general that it seems to fit almost anyone. As a Gemini, I know all about the split personality, the desire to travel, etc. Very soon she started into my background — parents, sister, and other relatives. She told of early childhood incidents that were remarkably true. She then talked about my relationship with my wife and children, and their individual personalities and traits. It was uncanny how she hit it right on the head. Then, she went into very specific things that would happen to me in the next few years.

I doubted some of them at the time. But every single one actually did happen. These things were told to me over a two-hour period with her eyes shut while holding my hands.

In a trance-like state, she began to relate how I had needed to build a place in the deep forest and had done that to repay a debt that occurred in one of my past lives. In the fourteenth century, I was a Jesuit Priest in France. My boldness and frank assertiveness resulted in being branded a heretic. It was necessary to escape to save my life. I snuck out into the forest and walked for many days until I came upon an old hermit who took me in. He fed me and nursed me back to good health. There were many things about the forest and nature that he taught me. When I left, in gratitude I vowed to some day repay him for what he had done for me, and it was in this lifetime that I chose to pay back this karmic debt.

Obviously there is no way for me to know whether or not any of this is true. But who knows? Maybe all of the people who find pleasure in their visit to the Hostel in the Forest owe it all to that fourteenth century French hermit!

HOSTEL MANAGERS
AND GUESTS

Even though, I am the legal owner of the Hostel, I feel that it is really owned by the hostelers. They certainly run it, and so much of the credit for the success goes to the managers. After the first three, all of the rest have been hostelers who have agreed to stay on for a few months and run the place. They have contributed their talents and good energies in doing construction work, maintenance, and keeping the guests happy. It always amazes me that we have never been without a manager.

Every time one gets ready to leave, it has been easy to find a replacement. I tell them only to stay as long as they have enthusiasm. When it wanes, it is time to bring in new energy.

The only time I can remember a close call was when Neal was preparing to go back to school; we were down to the wire without a replacement. I was taking him to the bus at 2:00 that afternoon. At noon a car drove up. Neal looked out at a young Australian lad walking up the way. Before his foot touched the step, Neal blurted out, "How would you like to manage this Hostel?"

The startled expression on his face made us both think he might turn around and leave. It was Richard O'Hanlon, who not only turned out to be a great manager, but met his wife there. In fact, at least four managers have met their wives while at the

Hostel, and no telling how many of the hostelers have found their future mates there. There have been countless budding romances and many honeymooners who have occupied the tree houses. In fact, one of the managers proposed a passion tax for a manager's relief fund!

The first few years, the managers received no pay, and even now it is hardly sufficient to buy their food. They tell me that they receive an abundance in nonmaterial wages.

There are an incredible number of interesting, adventuresome guests and many of them seem to derive a lot of pleasure from contributing to the success of the Hostel. They contribute their time and talent without compensation in helping both the managers and me. I am constantly astounded by the amount of talent passing through . . .

As I think back, there was Mark from Northern Ireland who, with a number of hostelers, built the new swimming pool and the storage shed. Tim spent timeless hours constructing the new kitchen. Burt orchestrated the parking lot to get the cars out of sight of the Hostel and enlarged the manager's room. Neal built the manager's room and original storage shed by himself. Lowell helped complete the first tree house, Clyde built the screen porch, and so many others did so much in tangible and intangible ways to make the Hostel what it is.

Not only must the manager keep the hostelers happy, maintain the building and grounds, but it is necessary to be a good organizer of social events. Some truly fabulous parties have taken place using the musical talents of the hostelers. Many of them have been professionals.

One woman was a flautist with the New York

Philharmonic. Twins from Melbourne, Australia, played the night club circuit back home with piano and guitar. A singer-guitarist from Sydney, Australia, landed a part-time job at one of the clubs on St. Simons. A jazz sax and a clarinet player performed one night by each being in the woods on opposite sides of the domes making sounds like you wouldn't believe. So many piano players and guitarists have gotten everyone in a party mood causing even the shy guests to break out in song.

I suppose I have been lucky enough to attend most all of these events. If someone were to ask me what was the best one, there are two that really stand out in my mind. Murray's bachelor party and David's birthday.

When Murray and Cathy, the local Girl Scout leader, agreed to tie the knot, Murray's friend, Heinz, from Munich, Germany, flew in to be the best man in the wedding. He was a typical Bavarian and a fun-loving frolicker. Somehow that night at the party no one had gotten around to eating much food, but the keg of beer was going fast. Meanwhile, we had prepared a skit which took place in the bunkroom.

Murray was laid out in a box made to look like a coffin. A funeral service was held with me acting as the minister. It was hilarious and naturally Murray was tossed into the pond at the end.

Another memorable fun party was when manager David Mitchener had a birthday. Loads of local friends like Bill and Gwen, Wendy, Billy, Selma, Murray and Cathy, and others joined in the festivities. The appearance of a keg of beer was usually an indication that everyone would be thrown into the pond before the night was over, and, sure enough, this was no exception. We sang and danced on into the night. Some of us guys even did a take-off skit on *Chorus Line*.

Since David was Australian, Wendy had made a huge chocolate cake sculptured in the shape of a kangaroo, which was not an easy feat. At some point during the wee hours, I was playing the piano, probably *Georgia On My Mind*. Murray came over with a finger full of chocolate that he claimed to have scraped from the cake. He stuck his finger in my mouth. As I started to chew, I ran out the door gagging. He had, instead, stuck his finger in David's jar of vegemite, a horrible substance made of rotten vegetables that all Australians eat.

THE LAW OFFICE PARTY

The people who work at my law office have learned to expect the unexpected from me. Many hostelers have walked the two blocks from the bus station to my office to leave their backpacks and wait for the old hostel truck to pick them up. They sit in our reception room in all manner of dress, and usually our receptionist can't understand a word they say.

A few years ago, we doubled the size of our law office by adding a second story. After spending six months in temporary quarters, we were happy to return to our newly renovated building and felt that a party for friends and clients was in order. A caterer was hired to prepare all of the fancy foods, and the office was decorated with a mass of flowers, etc. Instead of hiring a professional bartender, I offered to bring along a couple of hostelers for the job. Some of the partners were a little reluctant because they wanted this to be a swell affair with only the best of everything. As luck would have it, there were two Australian boys at the Hostel who claimed to have bartended on a cruise ship, and they even had their formal attire. I felt very pleased to let my partners know that we do have professionals at the Hostel; in fact, some of the best I know of anywhere.

Hundreds of people attended the gala event, and everything was cruising right along as planned. However, it seemed that our bartenders must have drunk one for every one they served. I began to hear rumors that they were telling a lot of "off-colored jokes." The place was so packed, it wasn't easy for me to get downstairs to check on them. I was continually greeting people and showing them around my upstairs office.

One of my partners came up to see me with a look on his face that let me know things were not all right. Apparently one of our clients, who walks on crutches, had gone into the office that had been converted into the bar and asked for a beer. The Aussies unbuttoned his shirt while he stood there speechless and poured the beer down the inside of his pants. For fun-loving Australians, they thought nothing of it. The way to have a good party is to really get down. Had it been a Hostel party, no one would have thought much about it, but at the law office it was a bit much. I went downstairs and admonished them to mind their manners.

Later in the evening, one of the senior partners came storming into my office, red in the face. He had taken his wife in for a drink and after properly preparing it, they poured it over her head. This was a blunder of major proportions. I called Burt, the manager, to come immediately and take them back to the Hostel. Since they were in no condition to drive, I had them incarcerated in my truck to await his arrival, but they kept escaping and were trying to pick up every female that walked by.

Needless to say, Australians have been banned from ever serving at another office party, and an eyebrow is raised whenever I even mention the availability of a hosteler to do any type of menial labor around the office.

PART 3

HOSTEL PURPOSE

Most males have incorrigible egos, and to this offense I plead guity. Perhaps it has something to do with fear of death. I'm really not sure. The fact remains that we are all mortal. Struggle as we might to search for bits of immortality, this body will someday be dust. So perhaps this Hostel thing with me is one giant, selfish, egocentric plot to have my memory live beyond my allotted time here on earth. But, if so, I have deceived myself into believing that there are truly altruistic intentions.

The most important goal we have on this earth, in my opinion, is to attain peace among all peoples. Ideally, we should love one another. But if we can't bring ourselves to the point of love, we should at least tolerate each other. How many times have I heard it said, and I've been guilty of it myself: "Germans are so and so . . ." "The English think they are . . ." "Can you believe the French, the way they act?" "The Americans now are really the . . ." We generalize so much about people who happen to be born within certain manmade borders. My God, we are still fighting the Civil War here in the South well over 100 years after we surrendered. But when an astronaut is in one of those space capsules and looks back at beautiful Mother Earth, he sees no borders whatsoever.

It is interesting to observe certain differences in people, depending on where they come from. But when it gets down to bedrock, we are all just alike. In so many of my travels, I have stayed in homes in countries such as Yugoslavia, Bulgaria, Romania, Hungary, India, Nepal, and Tibet. Wherever I may have sat down and talked with people by their firesides and eaten their food, I found that basically we are all just alike. We all have the need for survival, a love for family and children, a desire to eat a decent meal, share conversation, and we all want peace. It is reaching out and touching each other and feeling that even though you may live on the other side of the world, there is that same thing in you that makes you tick that I also have inside me.

The Buddhist may say that this merely is a communion of the spirit or soul that lies within us that binds us together. I don't think it is something that can be put into words. But you know it when you feel it. When I shake another person's hand and look into his eyes, there is something between us that says, "I am in here; are you in there?" Call it a kindred spirit or whatever, but it does give me the reassurance to have that sensation that we are all basically the same, if we can just look beyond skin color, language, and external habits. It is a bonding that I have felt during the years I traveled and met so many people who befriended me. This Hostel, to me, is, in a certain sense, my attempt to repay them. Maybe the psychic was right. Perhaps there are past karmic debts that I must attempt to repay.

I strongly believe that when hostelers gather

from all over the world to share a meal and talk, something happens that may not be obvious to them at the time. Sometimes we break through that invisible shield that all of us have surrounding us and find understanding. I am firmly convinced that a future prime minister of England, a future chancellor of Germany, and future leaders of other nations of the world have stayed or will stay at the Hostel in the Forest. And who knows? Perhaps as he or she ate a mullet and drank a beer with people from other countries, a piercing of the veil transpired. For one instant there may have been a communion of the spirit that will live with them the rest of their lives. Believe me, my friends, it is understanding that will bring about the peace that we all strive for.

I'm sure that my recounting these aspirations pale in comparison to some multilateral conference of national leaders. But a raging fire can start from one spark, and I'm crazy enough to have confidence that the spark might begin right here in this magic place.

Right up there in rank with world peace is protecting the environment. It is not just an ideal, it is a necessity that we make drastic changes in our lifestyles to advance the years of Mother Earth. I confess that as much as I would like to, we don't wholly adhere to these principles at the Hostel.

For example, I always wanted the place to make a statement for the environment, yet we have a big cement swimming pool. But God knows, it feels so good on a hot, summer day. We do strive to make the surroundings relatively natural. There is no artificial heat or air-conditioning. Heating is provided by an old buckstove, and cooling by an electric fan. We make efforts to recycle all waste and have a compost pile. But then we have water-flushing toilets. We heat our hot water by gas rather than solar, and there are many other compromises. But to most people, it seems that we are isolated in nature. That bumpy road winding one-half mile back to the parking lot is intentional.

Someone may speed down the interstate at 70 to 80 mph, turn off at Exit 6, down Highway 82 to the little pathway that leads to the Hostel, and get awfully aggravated that the holes in the road slow them up. "You should do something about that road!" they chide me.

I just smile. The whole idea of this place is to slow down your lifestyle. This is a place where you can spend a few days getting your head back together from the bustling world out there. So many have come for one night and stayed for several. The guest book where hostelers write their feelings about the place speaks louder than anything I might say.

Occasionally, a hosteler will also sense that magic, the same peace and tranquillity I felt on that fateful day when I wandered down the animal path to this little clearing. Many of them have attempted to describe their feelings to me or to write it in the guest book.

When Jaxon Hice first joined our construction team in building the Hostel, he spent several nights in the domes all alone. Or was he? He recalled:

> "I moved to the Hostel the day I was hired and lived outside. My bedroll was spread on a stack of plywood under the Spanish moss. The nights were beautiful and quiet. I would go into the domes and play my shakahatchi flute. The acoustics were amazing. The swamp was filled with every registry of sound.

"One full-moon night in late winter, after I had finished playing and was sitting in meditation, every owl in South Georgia came to the domes. There were at least seven or eight different species and as many as fifty or sixty individuals. They all started screeching and hooting as if in recognition of my presence. It sounded like a horologist shop on the hour. They kept up the cacophony for about a half hour, then dispersed as mysteriously as they had arrived."

Some weeks after I visited the psychic, she came to the Hostel ostensibly because her son was going to Europe and needed a hostel membership card. She told me that while at the Hostel, she saw gnomes and wood nymphs in the trees and other good spirits of the forest.

"That is a good sign," she said. "They will guard it and protect it from harm."

I thought of that statement a few years ago when I got the dreaded call at my office I had hoped I would never get.

The manager cried out, "There's a wildfire and it's heading our way!"

We are totally vulnerable to fire, which is why we can't buy any insurance. Just a couple of months previously, I had been terribly upset that our local papermill had clear-cut the property adjacent to our parking lot. Prior to that, it was a beautiful forest with cypress ponds. Then, they totally devastated it.

Well, anyway, the flames were leaping to the tops of the trees and was totally uncontrollable. A strong wind was blowing in our direction, but when the wildfire reached the clearing, the firefighters with trucks of water were able to put it out. Sometimes what we perceive as being bad can turn out to be good.

In America, we have less than ten percent of the world's population, yet we consume more than 60 percent of the world's resources. Sometimes I liken America's policy toward the environment to an old-fashioned Southern fish fry. When I was growing up, we lived near the Ocmulgee River, and some friend or family member was always fishing. Usually channel cat fish were caught which gave rise to inviting all the friends and neighbors to share in the catch. Somehow I can visualize my uncle saying to the multitudes, "We have 300 fish and 300 people, so each person gets one fish a piece." I can just imagine what he would say and do if some whippersnapper came along and put ten fish on his plate, and then his smart-aleck friend grabs eight for himself. Obviously somebody's going to be left out.

Why is it that we use the Earth's resources like there is no tomorrow? There's no harm in living a life where we share with everyone else. Why are we so greedy? Our children, grandchildren, and great-grandchildren are entitled to a happy and useful life. What will they say about our generation 100 years from now? We are polluting the Earth for our own selfish gain and leaving it to those who come after to deal with our mistakes. We need to think more of them and less of us. It has been said that a sign of maturity is when we give more than we take from the world.

"Plant the seed of the tree under whose shade you may never sit."

I hope, in spite of our environmental compromises, that the people who visit the Hostel in the Forest will have an opportunity to observe and learn something from Mother Nature. Perhaps what we have here is an experiment to see if man and nature can live in harmony with each other. I want to always be aware of the need to conserve and preserve the Hostel's beauty for future generations to enjoy.

There really is something special here. I'm not quite sure what it is. I remember a German boy sitting on the deck talking to other hostelers about his inability to leave. They all agreed that there must be some kind of invisible trap. A new backpacker came walking up the road and the German sighed, "Well, here comes another victim."

So that brings us back to where we started. Why a hostel?

No, Mama, I shouldn't have built it. You're right. Other lawyers make money from their investments. I also agree with you that I will never have a penny because I throw it all away. But, Mama, if you must know, I'm having a damn good time doing it.

MANAGERS FOR
THE HOSTEL IN THE FOREST

Harry Kaufman	USA	Jul 75 - Sept 75
Parker Mullis	USA	Oct 75 - Jan 76
Bryan Parker	USA	Jan 76 - Jan 77
Lowell Nottingham	USA	Jan 77 - Apr 77
Barbara Rosenberg	USA	Apr 77 - Jun 78
Gerit Van Grol	Holland	Jul 77 - Jun 78
Steve Tanner	USA	Jun 78 - Aug 79
Manfred Bleif	Germany	Dec 78 - Jun 79
Roger Bowen	Australia	Aug 79 - Nov 79
Murray Wilson	England	Sept 79 - Oct 81
Sybille Russius	Germany	Nov 80 - Aug 81
Jimmy Guess	USA	Jul 81 - Sept 81
Rowan Frost	Australia	Sept 81 - Jan 82
Natalie Sexton	Australia	Sept 81 - Jan 82
David Mitchener	Australia	Jan 82 - May 82
Neal Gifford	USA	May 82 - Aug 82
Richard O'Hanlon	Australia	Aug 82 - Nov 82
Helen Mahoney	Australia	Sept 82 - Jan 83
Jerry George	Canada	Jan 83 - Apr 83
Patty Smith	USA	Jun 83 - Aug 83
Eric Bates	USA	Apr 83 - Oct 83
Sean Holohan	Australia	Oct 83 - Dec 83
Rob Rencen	New Zealand	Dec 83 - Feb 84
Katrina Rennecke	Germany	Apr 84 - Jun 84
Arthur Weeden	Australia	Jun 84 - Nov 84
Jacques de Broekert	USA	Nov 84 - Jan 85
Thomas Wagner	Germany	Jan 85 - Mar 85
Lyse Savard	Canada	Jan 85 - Mar 85
Hugh O'Donnell	Australia	Mar 85 - Aug 85
Jo Ann Vincent	England	Mar 85 - Aug 85
Pablo Bernal	Columbia	Aug 85 - Feb 86
Tim Baumberg	Canada	Dec 85 - Jan 88
Burt Weasel	USA	Dec 87 - May 88
Silla Vogt	Germany	Jan 88 - May 88
Mark Gribbin	Northern Ireland	May 88 - Sept 88
Heike Schmitt	Germany	May 88 - Sept 88
Zophie Pacek	Australia	Sept 88 - Dec 88

David Kyle	Canada	Sept 88 - Jun 89
Ted Dennard	USA	Jun 89 - Jan 90
Peter Walsh	Ireland	Jan 90 - May 90
Marty Walsh	USA	Jan 90 - May 90
Kathy Evans	England	May 90 - Dec 90
Paul Gregson	England	May 90 - Dec 90
Jeff Dennard	USA	Dec 90 - Jun 91
Pete Hannon	USA	Jun 91 - Nov 91
Clyde Jones	USA	Nov 91 - Jun 92
Jim McCarthy	USA	Jun 92 - Feb 93
Jennifer Hanan	USA	Jun 92 - Feb 93

CHOMOLUNGMA

Photo: Mount Everest

CHAPTER 2

CHOMOLUNGMA

"Vegetable curry? Sir, you order vegetable curry, no?"

The sound and fury of that word "Curry," pulled me out of a deep sleep. Barely able to focus my eyes, the pretty Indian flight attendant crept into view.

"Sorry to wake you, sir. You want vegetable curry?"

"Of course, I love curry."

She handed me the tray which did not appear too appetizing or maybe it just lacked the presentation. It was very obvious that I needed to get myself out of the sleep state. I think I had been dozing practically all the way from London. Normally sleep doesn't come easy for me on a plane, but it had been a long time since I had seen a bed.

The couple seated next to me were Sikhs returning to India after drumming around Europe in an attempt to sell their handmade leatherwares. I must have fallen asleep as we were talking about the religious differences among the Hindus, Sikhs, and Muslims who try to co-exist in Northwest India. It's not easy for them. The feelings continue to run deeply, but my body was too tired for much intellectual conversation.

Without hesitation, they began to devour their

lunch. The food I ate in the London Airport stole my appetite, and anyway it seemed like a good idea to let this curry set for a moment. Perhaps it would help to blend it.

In making a survey of all the people on this packed flight, I didn't see anyone who appeared to be from a Western country except me. Most certainly, I seemed to be the only American on this 747. But what does one expect on an Air India flight from London to Delhi? This just made the trip even a little more exciting, since I was heading into a different part of the world, an area I had longed to explore. Having already reached the maximum amount of hype for this trip, I still had these tingling feelings in the pit of my stomach that seemed to make the excitement grow even larger.

It would be nice if that pretty Indian girl would bring me something to drink, I thought.

My mouth was dry. They say that when flying it is necessary to prevent dehydration by drinking a lot of liquids. Not alcohol, though, because that has a tendency to dry the body out even more. You certainly don't need to have a hangover to add to the fatigue of jet lag.

I took my first bite. "What in the —?" Before I could even think, I jumped from my seat and ran down the aisle to the toilet. Fortunately, there were no obstructions. Believe me, I have been eating Indian foods for 20 years and, even before that, my father's hot barbecue sauce, but this curry took the cake. How is it possible for them to serve food that hot on an airplane?

After getting my mouth washed out with water, which incidentally does nothing to stop it from burning, I returned to my seat. All around me, the passengers were gobbling up their food like it was some mild chicken broth. Sitting down, I smiled my apologies to my neighbors.

Tom, old boy, I told myself, you're in a different culture. You may think you are well-traveled and urbane, but Europe and America are quite different from this part of the world.

I sat back and pulled out the flight map from the seat pocket. This 15-hour flight was to be interrupted only by a stop-over in Kuwait and Dubai.

Kuwait sits on the northern portion of the Persian Gulf. Dubai is one of the United Arab Emirates and is located on the southern point of the Persian Gulf. I have read these names in the news many times, but yet they still feel so far away. I never really expected to set foot in either country.

The flight attendants gathered up the trays. They probably used the leftovers to help fuel the plane. *Chariots of Fire* was the inflight movie, certainly appropriate for this flight. Anyway, I had seen it twice, so I leaned back in my seat to practice a little introspection.

This was without a doubt the most exciting trip of my life. I had already made 12 trips to Europe, backpacking around, and eventually made it to every country there. Doing a lot of mountain hiking and photography always brought about great excitement. But this one was the biggest of all — the Himalayas.

For so many years, I had wanted to go there. Looking at pictures, I often would drool over their luring enchantment, being mesmerized by their beauty and charm. It had become my lifetime dream and progressed into an obsession.

It always made me smile when I would think of my first mountain adventure. It started on a Norwegian train from Oslo to Bergen in 1975 to visit an acquaintance whom I had met a few years earlier in southern Italy.

It is normal for me to get tired of sitting; I usually walk around to do a little people-watching. On this train, two big Norwegians (one 6'6", the other 6'5") struck up a conversation with me. Both had just graduated from law school, and they were delighted to find a young lawyer from America. They were extolling the virtues of mountain-hiking and encouraged me to join them.

I first declined. Then, reluctantly I decided to go along to see what it was about.

We stayed the first night in a hostel in Finse, Norway, and the next morning started the ascent into the mountains. It was August, the most hateful month of the year in Georgia with its draining heat and high humidity, but in Norway the snow was falling. I tried desperately to back out because I only had T-shirts and a light jacket. But they wouldn't take "no" for an answer and found some warm clothes for me. We had to wade across streams of freezing water, and I was convinced that one had to be crazy to do a thing like this.

In the mountains of Norway, there are cabins located about six-hours hiking distance apart. They are equipped with bunk beds and a wood stove. The kitchen is stocked with canned goods brought in by helicopter. This saves considerably on the gear, since you don't have to pack tents, food, etc. It works on an honor system, and the ecology-minded Norwegians made sure that no one took advantage of it. We, like the other hikers, felt compelled to leave the cabin cleaner than we found it and deposited a little extra money in the wooden box in case we forgot to write down everything we ate. It amazed me that a system like that could work so well. Unfortunately, it probably wouldn't in the United States.

The second day we hiked up to a large glacier, went inside it, and laid our hands on the blue ice. After reaching the top of the mountain, we gazed more than a mile down into the spot where the vast Hardangerfjord begins. It was the most spectacular natural beauty I had ever seen, and to have walked up there under my own steam made me appreciate it even more. Before our hiking days ended, I was hooked.

When I returned to the island of St. Simons off the coast of Georgia, my home since law school graduation, I wasted no time in getting backpacks for my wife, three kids, and myself. We headed up to the Appalachian Trail in northern Georgia, so I could introduce them to this new experience. Since that time, we have hiked many a mountain in Europe and North America. There is no better way to enjoy nature and learn to appreciate this beautiful Earth that God created for us. But like other hikers, the big granddaddy of all mountains loomed in the back of my mind.

The tallest mountain in the world is Mount Everest, located on the border of Nepal and Tibet. I had hiked the Alps in Switzerland, Italy, Germany, and Yugoslavia; the Tatra Mountains, which separate Poland from Czechoslovakia; the Appalachians and the Cumberlands in the Eastern U.S.; the Rockies and Sierra Nevadas in the West; the mountains of Baranoff Island near Sitka, Alaska; and others. But none of them hold a candle to that old biggy in the Himalayas. The Rockies in Colorado look huge, but you are talking 14,000 feet or so. Mt. Everest is 29,028 feet.

I had no idea how much of it I could do, but I

wanted to go as high as my body would allow.

My family encouraged me to go for it. That old biological clock ticked loudly inside me, and I have always wanted to do it all before going on to my reward. I just don't want to miss anything. When a man passes 40, he begins to think a lot about the fact that a great deal more life is behind him than ahead of him.

At last, the flight attendant brought drinks. It was welcomed to help cool down my insides. The Sikh companions were stretched out in their re-clined seats and slept until our refueling stop in Kuwait.

Earlier, I had told them of this dream of mine to trek in the great Himalayas. It was November, the best month of the year to see these mountains. From December until Spring, there is much snow with bitter cold. Then melting snows and avalanches pre-cede the summer monsoons. Mid-to-late autumn is notoriously the time photographers dream of when there are bright cloudless skies.

For the previous five years, something had caused a delay in making this trip. First, there were prob-lems of getting away from the law office for a month, then cash shortages, and more recently I did not feel that I was in peak physical shape.

The trek up to Mount Everest demands your best. At the beginning of the year, I was beginning to psych myself up for the big event when a serious deterrent sprang up. One cold January night, I ran into the health center to work out. Being in a hurry, I foolishly did no stretching or warming up and did a real number on my lower back.

Agony is not a strong enough word for my feel-ings. The physical pain was bad enough but enduring the mental anguish of another setback in my plans was too much.

Steve Saul, my chiropractor friend, got me running again by May. After being out of training for four months, I had to really dig down for that extra bit of self-discipline. It was necessary to run longer distances, swim extra laps, and add a little more weight to the Nautilus machines. This meant setting the alarm about an hour and a half earlier than normal, and this continued almost daily until the day of the flight.

After a one-hour refueling stop in Dubai, we deplaned. The crew cautioned all passengers that no one must take any bag off the plane that contained alcohol. They warned that we would be thoroughly searched since all alcoholic beverages are strictly forbidden in the Arab countries. After the customs search, many of the passengers ran over to one section of this very large and modern duty-free shop. Thinking that the hot curry had caused a rush on the restroom, I sauntered over to that area to find, much to my shock and dismay, a gigantic liquor store. The Arabs really have an eye for business. They would no doubt jail you if you consumed any booze in the country, but have no qualms or reservations at all in the amount they are willing to sell you. Life is full of ironies and paradoxes, *n'est pas*?

Prior to this, hiking for me had mostly been on mountains less than 7,500 feet. The trek up to Everest begins at 10,000 feet. In reading books on Himalayan trekking, I found out that there are many more dangers that a hiker would encounter at higher altitudes. The higher someone goes, the more the body becomes oxygen-starved.

A friend sent me a book called *Medicine For Mountaineering*. It told in gory detail what happens to the body at high altitudes and that most everyone will experience different degrees of such symptoms: headaches, dizziness, fatigue, shortness of breath, loss of appetite, nausea and vomiting, disturbed sleep, attacks of anxiety, and irregular breathing. I had already begun to have a lot of these symptoms just thinking about them, especially those anxiety attacks.

I also read and brought with me *A Guide To Trekking In Nepal* by Stephen Bezruchka which is an excellent book. He has a chapter on the various health and medical problems that one will experience. This bothered me considerably, because I go to extreme efforts to stay healthy and keep my body in good physical condition. These books say that altitude sickness can be fatal. Many have died from not heeding the warnings. It is essential that when one climbs above 10,000 feet, it is necessary to ascend gradually and allow the body to acclimatize. Experts advise that you sleep no higher than 1,000 feet from where you slept the night before. It is also necessary to allow some rest days where no hiking is done at all.

Another way to survive is to drink lots of fluids to prevent dehydration. The very serious climbers not only know the exact amount of liquid intake, but they also measure the volume of their urine. One must drink no less than four quarts of water per day, which has to be purified with iodine tablets or filtered, or boiled, which should produce at least one quart of colorless urine. If it has a yellowish tint, then you are not drinking enough. Also, alcohol is a no-no at high altitudes.

When I read the list of medications that Bezruchka recommended carrying, it would have required an extra backpack. He reckons that one should take moleskin, bandages, a thermometer, water purification chemicals, leech repellent, iron pills, nose spray, decongestants, antihistamines, aspirin, codeine, drugs for diarrhea and dysentery, antibiotics, sunscreens, eye drops, malaria suppressants, and miscellaneous scissors, needles, safety pins, forceps, and tweezers. I thought that surely this guy must be a hypochondriac, and so I refused to adhere to his advice of carrying along a portable hospital. If all of that was necessary, then I wasn't going.

Ironically, while I was working so hard to get my body in shape prior to leaving, there were a slew of inoculations that were required before entering Nepal. It seemed that everyday I visited the health department for an injection against such loathsome diseases as polio, tetanus, diphtheria, tuberculosis, cholera, typhoid, infectious hepatitis, and malaria. It seemed so contradictory to my preparations for body-training because each one always set me back a little.

Taking this trip had certainly not been without some fear and trepidation on my part, but I tried to conceal that from my family. They encouraged me to do it; they knew how much it meant to me, except my mother who continued to chide me as if I were a little boy. "Why go off somewhere to climb mountains? Why don't you take normal vacations like everyone else? Why do you always stretch things to the limit?"

My retort would be, "But, Mama, there are certain things in life that I need to do. I like adventure. I like to meet new and interesting people."

She would usually have the last word by saying, "But you have a wife and three children to be concerned about."

I have always been more than concerned about my wife and kids. But I am constantly lured by the beauty of God's Earth. There are so many places in the world to see, and I would like to get around to visiting as much of it as I can. What can be wrong with trying to live out some of my fantasies?

The saving grace with my mother was former President Jimmy Carter. Whatever he says is the gospel with her. So fortunately for me, President Carter and Rosalyn had just taken this same identical trip and arrived back in Plains, Georgia, in good health two days before my departure.

Carlton Hicks who lives on St. Simons Island is a friend from college days when I was dating a girl from his home town of Perry, Georgia. Carlton is a close personal friend of Jimmy and Rosalyn, and he called them the morning after their return from the Himalayas.

Jimmy Carter very graciously phoned me and spent about 20 minutes giving me advice. There were men in his party who had completed the iron-man competition in Hawaii, had run marathons, and were in tip-top shape, but because of altitude sickness, all in his party had to be helicoptered out. He and his Sherpa guide were the only ones to make it all the way up to Kala Pattar at 18,500 feet. This spot supposedly offers some spectacular views of Mount Everest. He cautioned me to descend immediately if I felt any symptoms of altitude sickness. All of his Secret Service men had trained for this trip at Pikes Peak, Colorado, but none of them were able to complete the trek. He told me about a party of Germans who had been swept away by an avalanche and a group of hikers from India who were blown off the mountain by 200 mph winds. On the last leg of his trek, he was in snow up to his shoulders.

I don't think Rosalyn was very enamored with

this trip. She contracted altitude sickness at Namche Bazaar and never got beyond this village at 11,500 feet. Anyway, he ended the conversation with something like, "I hope you have fun and I wish you the best." When he hung up, I heard my daughter, Susan, and Juanita, who helps us clean, screaming down in the kitchen. They had listened in on the extension and were ecstatic over listening to the former President talking to me on the phone.

However, after hearing all of the perils, they were not so thrilled about me taking this trip. My mother, who didn't know the contents of the conversation, was pleased now because I told her that Jimmy and Rosalyn had just made this same trip and what a good time they had.

Since I was leaving the next day, I had to begin psyching myself out of any fear. I had read that altitude sickness is like sea sickness in that it has nothing to do with what kind of physical shape one is in. Some of the strong, young jocks are the ones who get the sickest. As long as the symptoms are mild, there is no cause for alarm. Knowing that the highest and most beautiful mountains in the world are there made someone like me continue on. I had decided that my constant prayer would be, "If Jimmy Carter can do it, then I can, too."

Obviously, a trekker can throw on the pack and hike up to Everest without a guide. There are Sherpa Tea Houses to toss the sleeping bag, and they will even feed you for a very small fee. But I had promised my family that I would use a trekking company in case something unforeseen came up. Some of the expensive ones cater to the elite who don't want to rough it too much. Porters are furnished to carry the packs, tent, food, and whatever one fancies to take along. Never in my life had anyone carried my pack, and the whole idea sounded repugnant.

These trekking companies do cut through all of the governmental red tape by getting the required permits and the like. They also are experienced in dealing with altitude sickness and other problems that a trekker may encounter. But traveling with a group is my idea of what hell must be like.

The only time I ever traveled with a group was when Marie and I were in Greece. We took a five-day group tour of the Peloponnese. An older couple from New York bitched and moaned and complained about everything imaginable during the entire trip and made everyone else miserable. So I have had the idea that there is a rotten apple in all groups that spoil the whole barrel.

Of all of the people that I have met in hostels, the Australians seem to be the most laid-back and re-laxed. Marie's travel agency found a good Australian company called Peregrine. Just like the name, they plan trips for people who like to rove and wander around like a falcon. It just so happened that they had an Everest trip scheduled for November 7th which fit perfectly into my plans.

As the plane was flying toward India, I closed my eyes and started recounting the items in my duffel bag such as long-johns, heavy ragwool socks, the sweater Marie knitted for me, my down jacket, wool hat, my Danner hiking boots, and the new sleeping bag graded to minus 5. Surely, I thought, I should be warm enough when we get up in the mountains.

My mind was flitting around like a drunken mon-key. President Carter's words were recalled: "If you get to the Pheriche Clinic, which is near the base camp, there's an American girl working there named Kathy

Olsen. If you see her, give her a big hug for me."

My mind then jumped to the remarks of my secretary. "I hate to be dumb, but can you tell me where in the heck is Nepal?"

All of my study of maps and my passion for the Himalayas made me assume that everyone should know exactly where it is.

"It is a relatively small country between the northern border of India and the southern border of Tibet," I answered smugly.

"Well, I don't keep up with places like that," she retorted. "If you don't tell me about it, how will I ever know!"

"Okay. Katmandu is the capital and is on the same latitude as Miami. Eight of the ten highest mountains in the world are located in the Khumbu region of Nepal. The southern part of the country has no mountains and is subtropical with jungles. The Chitwan National Park is in this section. That is where you ride into the park on an elephant and see tigers, monkeys, and other animals. The south also has great river-rafting trips on some of the world's best white water. But for me, the most spectacular attraction in the entire country is the beautiful snowcapped Himalaya Mountain range along the northern border."

"And that's where you're going?"

"Yep, Up in the Khumbu region where you see a lot of Buddhist temples."

"They worship Buddha over there?"

"In the north, they do, although the south of Nepal is predominantly Hindu."

I began to think of some of the things I had read about the country. Even though it has spectacular scenery, it has so many problems. It is the country with the highest illiteracy rate in the world, the lowest per capita income, the highest infant mortality rate, the highest percentage of population growth, and many diseases that we hear about but never experience. Agriculture is not sufficient to produce enough food to eat, and they have terrible deforestation problems. The fact that they don't replace the trees cut for firewood and building materials causes serious erosion.

Nepal was completely shut off to foreigners and any foreign influence until the 1950s. Most everyone knows that Sir Edmund Hillery from New Zealand and his Sherpa guide, Tenzing Norgay, were the first to climb to the top of Mount Everest in 1953. However, it was not until the 1960s before tourists began to appear, so trekking by Westerners is a relatively new thing to these people. It has really been only the previous years that the adventuresome have begun arriving in Nepal and exploring its beautiful surroundings. More people have yearned to see the highest mountain in the world named for Sir George Everest, the head of the survey team of India in 1823 who discovered that this mountain was actually the world's tallest. "Sagarmatha" is the Nepalese name for Mount Everest, meaning "Head of the Seas." However, I prefer the Tibetan and Buddhist name which is "Chomolungma," meaning "Goddess Mother of the World."

Nepal is just about on the opposite side of the world from where I live in Georgia. It is the first time I have ever had to make a decision whether I would fly to my destination in an eastern or western direction. I could have flown to Dallas and picked up Thai Air to Seattle, Tokyo, Bangkok, and Katmandu. Instead, it was a little cheaper (namely $1250 round trip) to go by New York to London to Delhi then to Katmandu.

There was no way for me to really sleep on that plane. I had too many butterflies in my stomach. It was almost 5:00 a.m. Delhi time when the captain announced that we were about to land.

The Delhi Airport was a sight to behold. Four other big 747's landed about the same time we did. There was British Air, Air France, Lufthansa, and Pan Am. All of the passengers were herded onto buses to transport us to the terminal. It turned out to be a race to see which bus driver could get there first. We were running neck and neck between the bus on the right and the one on the left. The bus to our right won by a shoulder as we skidded into the area in front of the terminal. At 5:00 a.m., this will certainly get the adrenalin flowing so there is no need for coffee. After that, one needs a drink to calm down.

There were perhaps 2,000 people on the five planes, and there was one man sitting at a small table to check each passport. He awkwardly arranged a line of chairs on both sides of the table extending them to the walls, to prevent anyone from attempting to by-pass him. For Americans, who are so demanding of efficiency, this requires an exercise in patience or perhaps even Zen meditation. It certainly gives one ample time to complete the landing card. It was already very warm and humid. The sun was about to dawn to make it much hotter since there was no air-conditioning. Everyone was tired and not at all ready to put up with Indian bureaucracy. I have been told that the British introduced bureaucracy to India and the Indians have perfected it.

I chatted with some of my disgusted neighbors in the long line. One couple was from Toronto. He was a medical doctor, also headed for Katmandu, and planned to hike up to some of the Nepalese mountain villages to treat the sick with his modern medicines. Most of the people in those areas have only been exposed to the "root doctors" who use various herbs, tree bark, and roots. For more serious problems, there are Shamans who stand by the sickbed chanting and beating their drums for hours to drive out the evil spirits.

My duffel bag had only been checked to Delhi, but the Indian official wouldn't let me pick it up because I didn't have a visa to enter India. A very nice man wearing a British Air name tag helped me break through the red tape. It is absolutely amazing what can happen when there is someone who dares to assume the authority to remove the hassles. He led me into a room full of bags that were in every possible manner of disarray. Eventually, I found the old olive drab army bag purchased from the Famous Store in Brunswick, Georgia. It had someone else's name and serial number printed on it, but it looked good to me because it was mine.

The next step was to proceed to the departure terminal in the adjacent building. It was like a warehouse with no offices or counters where you would expect to see the name of the airline you intended to fly. One woman in street clothes walked up to me and asked me where I was going. I thought she was tring to hustle me or maybe was just being nosy. Other people began walking in, so this woman pulled a stool from the corner out into the middle of the floor and proceeded to check us in. She tagged our bags and told us to go over to a booth in the corner to be checked out by customs. Watching the woman leave the building made us all feel a bit insecure; our bags were randomly strewn about the floor with no one around to care for them.

Being a Westerner, I guess I expected more. After all, Delhi is the capital city of India.

There were about a dozen people aimlessly wandering about hoping to find someone to ask about the Nepalese Airline. After what seemed like an eternity, the custom officials arrived. Separating the men from the women, they led us to a curtained-off booth. Each of us entered and stood on a box while being thoroughly frisked. They patted me down generously all over my body without any shyness. A woman passenger walked out of the adjacent booth complaining that the customs man was getting very familiar with his frisking. We both agreed that at this hour of the morning who cares. Since both booths had male customs officials, I never did figure out why they separated the men and women. Oh, well . . . Welcome to India!

The little twin-engine plane was filled to capacity. We taxied town the runway and took off into billows of cumulous clouds. Shortly, the clouds parted and we were treated to a sight I shall never forget, the great Himalayas sitting there in all their glory. Even though my tired body had been traveling for almost 40 hours, there is no way to describe the excitement I felt. There they were, looking like upside-down ice cream cones with vanilla topping. What a sight to behold!

Annapurna, the world's third highest mountain, came into view. All of the passengers moved to the left side of the plane to experience the spectacle of those mountains over 20,000 feet high. The flight through this fairyland was all too brief before landing in the hill country city of Katmandu. Though I was numb from fatigue, my body still permitted a few tingles. Thank God, I had made it to Nepal to experience my dream of a lifetime.

Just the name Katmandu brings on visions of eastern mysteries. It seemed exotic and brimming with intrigue. The little airport was filled with excitement because the King was departing. We watched the Mercedes limousine pull up to the single runway, and he boarded his private jet. There were officials lined up on either side to make a safe passageway for him.

The personnel at the airport were only slightly more organized than the Indians. Because it is so small, it didn't take too much time before I had my duffel bag in hand ready to set out for the hotel. Many young boys (who appeared to be no older than twelve) rushed up, pleading for me to ride in their taxis. I chose one little boy who was the most persistent and found that he drove a bedraggled old Fiat.

In Katmandu, they drive on the left side of the road with one hand on the steering wheel and the other on the horn. The streets were filled with people walking, riding bicycles, pushing carts, and old men hauling bales of hay strapped to their backs. There were cows roaming in the streets and just about anything else that you can think of. I wondered if the adventure of this taxi ride would overshadow the trek to Mount Everest.

I never knew that some countries break up their time zones in minutes rather than hours. Delhi was nine and one-half hours ahead of Eastern Standard Time, and Katmandu was one hour and ten minutes ahead of Delhi. Just before leaving home, we switched from Daylight Savings Time to Standard Time. Old John Lane, the eonian radio announcer for WMOG, told his listeners to move their clocks forward by one hour. After fifteen or so phone calls, he reversed himself and apologized that he meant to say backward one hour. Anyway, everyone at home was complaining about not being able to adjust to the one-hour change.

I couldn't help but imagine what the people at home would say if old John told them in his own inimitable way, "Well, tonight, folks, you must run your clocks back ten hours and forty minutes." That was the time difference I was going to have to deal with. It does take a while for the body to make that transition.

The precarious taxi ride ended at the surprisingly nice Shankar Hotel. It had been an old palace of some sort built in a French design. Seemingly there were hundreds of servants offering their services, including an old man in uniform who gave a hand salute as he graciously opened the door.

I was somewhat surprised to meet one of my traveling companions for the trek. Her name was Mary and was a very healthy, hearty 31-year-old from Melbourne. Her leg muscles looked like she played for the Chicago Bears, and I was told that she was a marathon runner. At six feet, she was taller than we two males of the group.

I immediately sized her up as a pretty tough cookie. If any of us could make this trip up the mountain, I would put my money on her. She was an industrial therapist by trade and seemed to have a no-nonsense, friendly attitude.

George, on the other hand, the other member of our trio, was a bit scrawny. I would not have picked him out of a line-up as being a jock. He was also 31-years-old and was born in England where he lived

until eight years ago. As a geologist, he had found work
in Sydney. He likewise was a runner and seemed to be
a nervous sort. I was the senior member of the
group, and what I lacked in physical strength, I
made up for it in stubborn determination.

Fortunately, the trekking agency took us all on a
tour of this ancient city that is thousands of years
old. It is filled with Buddhist temples and monuments. The Hindus outnumber the Buddhists, so
there are many ashrams as well.

A walk around the market place was a memorable experience. Throngs of people milled around.
Hunks of meat lay on the sidewalk almost obscured
by flies. Vegetables were in abundant supply — turnips, carrots, peas and cauliflower, and fruits like
oranges, limes, apples, mangos, and pomegranate. I
took lots of photographs to try to capture something
of the exotic mood of this area. It is a city not only
dominated by two religions, but also by divergent
lifestyles. For the wealthy tourist, there were fancy
hotels, The Yak and Yeti, Annapurna, and Shankar.
But a young backpacker would probably stay in the
Katmandu Guest House or the Blue Diamond Hotel.
There were nice restaurants like La Marmite, Old
Vienna, and Ghar A Kabab. There were numerous
Chinese eateries, if one preferred Oriental cuisine.

Being my first trip to Asia, the sights seemed
strange and mysterious to me; it was definitely not
for the weak-stomached. The smells were offensive
and not at all appetizing, and I had to constantly
watch where I stepped. Cows freely walked along the
streets, sidewalks, and anywhere else they had a
mind to go. I was told that it was a stiffer penalty to
kill a cow than a human. Because they give good
milk to drink and the fact that some Hindus believe

in transmigration, they are considered to be sacred animals. They are identified with the mother goddess. Besides the cows, there were a plethora of bicycle-driven rickshaws, Katmandu's answer to the taxi cab. Of the few cars on the streets, all blew their horns, creating a condition somewhere between chaos and bedlam.

We were told that we absolutely should not drink the water unless it was boiled or treated. "Never eat raw vegetables, peel all fruit, and eat only in clean-looking restaurants," was another admonition. Actually, the food was quite good. A lot of Indian curries were very tasty and not as hot as the food on that chariot of fire I flew on. The Nepalese use a lot of lentils which they call *daal*, poured over cooked rice, called *bhaat*. You can't go wrong ordering *daal bhaat* in most any eating establishment. Don't expect wine with the meal, but they did have a beer in a liter bottle. Dining in a good restaurant cost about $1.00 to $1.50, but beer was $2.00. One restaurant that catered to foreigners was Jamali's. While eating my lunch, I bit down on a piece of glass about the size of a quarter. I ran to the restroom and washed out my mouth. The waiter seemed totally unconcerned when I told him about it. He just shrugged his shoulders in a "so what?" gesture.

From the time of arriving in Katmandu, I had trouble sleeping. The altitude is only 4500 feet so that could not have been the reason. The most likely villain was the abundance of adrenalin that my body was pumping. Thank God for meditation.

One hour in a meditative state is better and more restful than many hours of sleep. The alarm clock in my brain would go off at 1:30 a.m. and, try as I might, sleep would not come. Since George was in the room with me, I would sneak out to a dark little sitting room and meditate until sunrise. One morning as I snuck back in the room, George raised up and asked if I had been out for a walk. I nodded. He surprised me by saying, "While you were out of the room, it gave me a chance to meditate." I felt relieved that I was with someone who understood the need and value of it.

The night before our departure to the Himalayas, the three of us went out to dinner to try to become better acquainted with each other. I came back feeling reassured that Australians are good traveling companions. It's not that I'm down on Americans, but we are so spoiled that it makes us more demanding. Invariably, there will be some American tourist complaining, griping, and bitching about everything. That spoils the trip for me.

The night before the trek was to begin, George and Mary felt inclined to go to bed early. But I was much too excited to go to sleep. The hotel lobby had a small bar. I ordered a Nepalese beer (about a 4 on a 10 scale), hoping that it would make me sleepy.

An older man was sitting there in deep conversation with the bartender. He wore one of the checkered hats that many of the Nepalese men wear. He looked at me and spoke in very good English, "Where are you from, sir?" He slipped over to the chair next to me and proceeded to tell me of his younger days in leading trekking parties in the Himalayas. It was obvious that he was an educated man and very well-read. When I asked him if he was Hindu or Buddhist, he surprised me by saying that he was a Christian.

"Are there many?" I asked.

"More than you might think," he replied.

He had converted from Hinduism to Christianity about 15 years previously. I was interested to know why he had done this. He told me of his conversion by a Christian missionary. We talked for quite a while about Himalayan trekking and religion. He invited me to his home to meet his family. It was not too far from the hotel.

He had a modest apartment on the second floor of a three-story building that would probably be considered plush by Nepalese standards. What impressed me most was his large collection of books. Many of them I had read. We talked for what seemed like hours before I realized I had a 5:30 a.m. wake-up call and had better get some rest.

DAY 1

Monday morning finally arrived. I didn't need that 5:30 a.m. wake-up call because I had been awake for over three hours. George and I made a last-minute check to see that everything was stuffed into our duffel bags. Both of us were as excited as two little kids on Christmas morning.

We hurried down to the hotel dining room and had breakfast with Mary. One of the fellows from the trekking company introduced us to our Sirdar, the head Sherpa guide. His name was Mailapemba.

For the first time, I learned that the Sherpas originally came from Tibet and appear much more Oriental. They are not as dark as the Nepalese, have rounder faces, and more slanted eyes.

The four of us jumped into a little Fiat taxi that seats about two less than we had in there. They couldn't shut the trunk, and our duffel bags were dangling out the back. At one point, I looked over my shoulder and couldn't see mine. Fear overcame me. I could visualize it falling into the middle of the street while hundreds fought over the contents. I felt uneasy until we arrived at the airport and saw that it was actually still hanging in there.

One disquieting event on the way to the airport was seeing a pedestrian who had been hit by a vehicle; he lay dead in the blood-splattered street. It brought me back down to earth to see this lifeless body. But the Hindus strongly believe that the body is only a shell or, as they say, an envelope. When the spirit leaves the body, the shell has no meaning, or when the letter is removed from the envelope, the envelope is discarded. Their strong belief in reincarnation assures them that this spirit will quickly find another shell to inhabit.

November is the height of the season for mountain hikers. The Katmandu airport was filled with would-be trekkers headed out for the high country. Lukla was our destination, the only airport in the Khumbu region, at 10,000 feet elevation. We nervously watched as the fog began to settle in. It could have been a long wait since each plane would seat only 14 people. Three flights were scheduled to leave at 8:30 a.m. for this 40-minute hop up to Lukla. One of the fellows from our trekking company was there. We were scheduled on the third plane, but somehow he arranged to bump us up to the second plane.

I didn't think anything about it at the time, but as it turned out, only two planes were able to depart that day. The third one couldn't find its way out of foggy Katmandu. So, this was the first of the many good omens and some of my Dennard luck. Marie tells me that I am the luckiest person she has ever known. Everything just always seems to happen right for me.

As the plane broke through the clouds, we were treated to a marvelous sight of the snowcapped Himalayan Mountains. I had to pinch myself over and over to make sure that it was real. I could never remember being so excited. This long-time dream was about to take place. I pressed my face against the window as we flew over the hill villages with a backdrop of gigantic, beautiful mountains. It was overwhelming.

The Lukla airport was an unnerving experience in itself. It had a very short and rocky landing strip on the side of a mountain at about a 45-degree angle. The plane landed at the edge of the cliff and taxied uphill toward a large stone wall. Somehow, the plane miraculously slowed down — just short of the wall — then made a right-angle turn and came to a jolting stop. I laughed out loud when I experienced this. No one in their right mind would fly into conditions like that.

As we were getting off, hordes of people ran up to the plane, trying to board. Droves of trekkers were trying to get out of Lukla. I talked with one American couple who had been waiting for five days. There were over 275 on the waiting list. They had not been able to get enough planes into Lukla because the weather was so foggy. Conditions have to be clear both in Katmandu and Lukla, as well as in between, or else the planes don't fly.

I found out that most people never chance this precarious flight at all and prefer to take a 13-hour bus ride from Katmandu to Jiri, which is a six-day hike from there to Lukla. If you take that route, you don't have to worry about the improbabilities of flying in and out. Another advantage of this is to begin trekking at a lower altitude so that you gradually acclimatize over the six-day period.

Once you reach Lukla, if there is fog, there is no way out except to walk. The Nepalese Army has a helicopter for $200 per person, but even it can't get in if there is fog. A party of Australians were split up; some of them were on the second flight with us and the rest were on the third plane that could not leave Katmandu. Their Sirdar was on the that plane, so they could do nothing except pitch their tents in Lukla and wait and hope that the plane would arrive the next day. If you're not into tent-sleeping, a few small guest houses or tea houses permit you to put your sleeping bag there for about 50 cents a night.

The weather felt so much colder at this higher altitude, and with no sun, we were all scurrying around for our duffel bags to pull out sweaters, jackets, wool hats, etc. After about half an hour, they served us a cup of hot tea which really hit the spot and helped us to warm up a bit.

All of a sudden, I started feeling a little dizzy and giddy-headed. I thought, Oh no! I can't start that right here at the beginning of the trip! I seemed to have a little tinge of nausea, too. I didn't want to tell anybody about it; I couldn't stand to think of feeling bad here at the very beginning of the trip. I had talked with several people who said that when they flew into Lukla, they always got a headache and nausea immediately. Maybe it as just the power of suggestion.

We were introduced to our head cook, Pema, and the assistant, Lhakpa. Mailapemba, Pema, and Lhakpa would be our Sherpa guides for the next fifteen days.

The Sherpas are the name of the people who live in the Khumbu region. They supposedly migrated

Pema

Lhakpa

Mailapemba

Namche Bazaar

into this region about a thousand years ago from Eastern Tibet. Isolated in these high mountain villages, they are probably not aware that they live in the most beautiful spot in the world. Life for them is about the same as it was centuries ago. There were no roads, no vehicles, no newspapers, no electricity, no telephones, or anything else that you can think of that was developed in the last several hundred years. They traveled strictly by foot on very narrow paths running up and down those steep mountains and across rivers from one little village to another.

Their one- or two-room mud huts had fires continually burning inside for cooking and warmth, but no chimneys to vent the smoke. When you entered these houses, the smoke hit you in the face. I found that pretty hard to get used to. Their beds consisted of wooden frames about three feet off the floor with a two- or three-inch cushion resting on the frame for a mattress. The mountain people had lots of children, and I'm sure the children must have slept on the floor.

It impressed me that these people were always smiling and had bright eyes that looked squarely into my eyes without any fear or any feelings of inferiority. They seemed to say, "You may look a lot different from me, being so tall, pale, round-eyed, lots of hair on your body, speaking that strange language, and wearing those fancy clothes, but basically down deep, we are all the same. We are one." I felt a strong energy from them that they didn't look up to me or down on me, but shared a true sense of equality. It was so refreshing to find this. They didn't have to say anything — their bright eyes told the story.

The cooks prepared our lunch, consisting of one fried egg, some potatoes, and sliced canned pineapple bought in Katmandu for us Westerners. It tasted pretty good to me; I was starved. After eating, my queasy feeling subsided, and I was ready to start hiking.

They brought along three porters who appeared to be about four-and-a-half feet tall and were packed like mules. They carried huge straw baskets almost as large as they were. Leather straps on the baskets fit around the tops of their heads, placing the weight on their foreheads.

These men could not have weighed a hundred pounds each, yet carried baggage on their backs far in excess of their weight. It made me feel guilty when I saw them burdened with 50-pound duffel bags, stacks of kitchen equipment, tents, and supplies on each of their backs. The only things we carried were day packs, cameras, and water bottles, so insignificant compared to their burden.

There were two sisters who also accompanied us, carrying much of the food on their backs. How was it possible for those little girls to carry such weight in those large baskets? They all seemed to be so happy and smiling, but it still made me feel bad.

As we started out on the trail, I met one little girl about three feet tall; she looked maybe eight years old. She had one of those huge baskets on her back full of cooking gear literally as big as she was and must have weighed twice as much as she did. I could only think that these sturdy people who have to balance so much weight on their foreheads must have awful neck problems.

In the beginning, the trail was very rocky. We had to keep our eyes on the path to prevent twisting an ankle. It was not easy for me to look down when I wanted to look up and see this magnificent scenery surrounding me.

The Dudh Kosi River flowed through the valley

to the west, and thick stands of pine and spruce trees grew up to the trail. Snow-covered mountains surrounded us. I can't describe the excitement I felt being there. It began drizzling rain, and the clouds descended upon us, blocking out that splendid view.

The Sherpas in the Khumbu are Buddhist. We saw many prayer wheels, white flags flying over houses and on poles, and Buddhist prayers inscribed on mountain walls. Their custom requires that one must always keep a prayer wall or any other Buddhist monuments on their right side. Fortunately, most prayer walls have a trail going on both sides. They believe that by spinning the prayer wheels, prayers could be sent in every direction.

It is also their belief that one's right side is masculine and the left is feminine. You must never touch food or any person with the left hand. This is not because of its femininity, but because they don't have toilet paper, and the left hand is used for cleaning yourself. It is an insult to violate their customs, so it is a good idea to be familiar with them. We were taught all of these things during orientation in Katmandu.

Along the trail, the Sherpas we met placed their hands together in prayer-like fashion and greeted us with "*Namaste*." This means I honor the God within you. I very quickly picked up on this and greeted everyone I met the same way. What a nice thing to say when you meet someone. They would always smile as they looked me right square in the eye. It made me feel so good to have such a warm welcome in this remote spot of the world.

In the beginning, the walk was relatively easy because we were descending in altitude from Lukla to a settlement on the Dudh Kosi River called Rokhumba, at about 8,000 feet. There was a small wooden house with an adjacent flat area for pitching tents. We entered the house to escape the drizzle, and it was packed with 15 or so hikers, mostly from Switzerland. They had been to Everest Base Camp and another place west of Everest called Island View. They complained about the temperature up there being 20 degrees below zero (F.) at night and about 15 degrees above during the day. It felt cold enough for me right there where we were. I was used to the warm, temperate climate of South Georgia. I had no idea what the current temperature was, but I was shaking all over. It really was my first exposure to cold weather in a long time.

They served us our first dinner inside the little wooden house. Our first course was a bowl of popcorn with a cup of tea. What a pleasant surprise! I love popcorn. The dinner consisted of potatoes, green beans, and some curry, with a little slice of cake. It looked good but I seemed to be feeling a little bit giddy. I was not interested in eating very much. Outside, the tiny drops of rain had turned to sleet. It was only 7:00 p.m., but I felt the need to go out to the tent and get in my sleeping bag to warm up and get some sleep.

I went to sleep immediately, but just as I had done the previous couple of nights in Katmandu, I woke up exactly at 1:45. No way could I get back to sleep. As is often the case at high altitudes, middle-of-the-night worries are the worst of all. I started going through my worst paranoia.

I remembered the Swiss hikers laughing at us when we told them we were headed up toward Everest Base Camp. They had attempted the climb through shoulder-deep snow, but the weather was so cold. I thought if these mountaineers from Switzerland couldn't make it, how was this South Georgia boy going to manage? Then I recalled all the horrible cases of altitude sickness I had heard tales about — one where they had gone to wake a man in his tent and found him dead. Suddenly, I was seized by a sense of panic and worst of all, a feeling of claustrophobia. I felt a sensation of being enclosed with no escape.

It seemed so crazy to be in wide-open spaces in the largest mountains in the world and feel claustrophobic. But I felt trapped. I knew if I turned back to Lukla, I would have to wait five or six days for a plane. If I continued onward, the weather would become colder and the likelihood of altitude sickness greater. I broke out in a cold sweat. I told myself, You've got to get hold of yourself! The best antidote is to counteract it with meditation. Miraculously, with God's help, the panic was calmed.

One of the things we were required to do was drink at least a gallon of water per day and more than that if possible. This somehow is a deterrent to altitude sickness by preventing dehydration. Drinking so much and with the extreme cold obviously makes it necessary to relieve yourself in the night. Being an experienced camper, I had prepared for that event by bringing along a plastic bottle. That is one great advantage that boys have over girls. I have learned to accomplish this feat without even having to get out of my warm sleeping bag.

But then, the worst of all calamities occurred. It had never happened before, but in putting the lid back on the bottle, I turned it over on top of my sleeping bag and pad. Poor George was sleeping right next to me. How revolting! This Australian would probably think that all Americans were crazy. I tried to clean it up with my T-shirt. Then I just didn't care anymore.

I lay awake for the rest of the night thinking about Mailapemba's suggestion that we do a full-day hike the next day up to Namche Bazaar at 11,500 feet. We had earlier planned only to hike a half-day. Everything that I had read about altitude sickness emphasized that it is necessary to acclimatize gradually. The faster you ascend, the more likely you are to get sick. I decided to make a plea to George and Mary to only go the half-day.

It was 5:00 a.m. and still dark, but I wanted to get out of my smelly sleeping bag and go outside. The tent flaps were frozen. The rain during the night had turned the tent into a house of ice. When I stepped outside, I was completely astounded. Looking up into the sky, I saw more stars than I had ever seen in my life. There was not a cloud in the sky, and it was totally illuminated with billions of bright lights. What a beautiful sight it was!

Sherpa porters along the trail

DAY 2

At 5:45 a.m., George crawled out of the tent for the fourth time. The poor guy had terrible diarrhea. He refused to take any medicine, saying that he wanted to wait and maybe it would get better on its own.

As dawn was breaking, I was delighted to see that clear sky again. We were surrounded by absolutely spectacular mountains that were hidden from view the day before. How could I have ever considered turning back? I felt so exhilarated. I pulled my sleeping bag out of the icy tent, unzipped it, and hung it over a rock wall to air out. It was amazing how much better I felt after the horrendous night of fear.

A hearty breakfast of oatmeal, eggs with onions, toast, and tea got me cranked up to tackle the trail. One can easily become spoiled by having someone else do the cooking, pitch the tents, pull the tents, clean the kitchen equipment, and break camp. In trying to rid myself of the guilt, I decided that this was going to be my luxury trip.

It was a cloudless, sunny day, and the mountains were incredibly gorgeous. As I walked the narrow trail, I stopped every few minutes to take pictures. We hiked along a beautiful, clear, raging river, the Dudh Kosi. The trail was very wooded, mostly pines and loads of rhododendrons. I would have liked to see them in bloom. It must be really beautiful in spring time.

The trail passed a one-acre Japanese-run vegetable farm, established to service the now defunct Everest View Hotel near Namche Bazaar. The garden had cabbage, carrots, turnips, onions, garlic, and potatoes. That stretch of the trail was spectacular.

After four hours, we stopped at Monjo for lunch.

Our group of three had its first disagreement. George argued that we should go on to Namche Bazaar, an extra four hours straight up the mountain with a 2,000-foot altitude gain. Mary and I tended to think it best to stay there for the evening and do some hiking around the area during the afternoon. George was very insistent, but Mary and I stood our ground. I was feeling great and could have easily walked another four hours, but I wanted to play it cautious with this altitude sickness. So many hikers we met coming down the trail told us horror stories about seriously ill people who had to be helicoptered out. The cardinal rule in dealing with the altitude problem is to take it easy. You should only ascend gradually each day.

That afternoon, I enjoyed short walks around the camp site and found a big flat rock to sit in the sun. I could see a small building not too far away that appeared to be a school. Young children were playing outside. Being led by an adult, they marched down the trail, playing little musical instruments, and singing. I later asked Pema about this, and he told me that it was the Hindu New Year. Even though there were only a very few Hindus in this area, they were enjoying their celebration.

The sun set behind the mountains by 4:00 p.m., and the temperature began to drop. I felt much better and was so happy to be there in such beautiful surroundings. The cooks were inside one of the houses preparing the meal. The barefoot porters built a campfire for themselves away from the tents. They laughed and played some kind of homemade board game that looked like checkers.

They always served us a nice hot cup of tea prior to supper to get us warmed up. The culinary delight of the evening consisted of mashed potatoes with tomato and onion sauce and Brussels sprouts. When you have hiked all day, any food tastes good, although a mountain trail is not a place that one expects to eat fine cuisine.

As per usual, we were inside our tents by 7:00 p.m. and ready for crawling in that sleeping bag to warm up. Normally, it takes me somewhere between five and ten seconds to go to sleep, but that night was unusual. I spent about four hours thinking, meditating, and tossing around.

I thought of my sweet wife and children. I wondered what they were doing. They were all so encouraging to me on this trip.

Susan had finished her French degree at the university and was at home. She and Marie had taken me to the airport. They both were so supportive. When Susan listened in on President Carter's call, she said, "You really do hold your own in talking with a President." I felt good about her and was very proud that she was going to work with Delta Airlines.

Then there was Ted, who was at the University of the South in Sewanee, Tennessee. He called me the morning I was leaving to tell me how much he loved me and what a bright spirit I was in his life. He always knows how to say the right things to me, and I felt really good about him, too.

I was also very proud of Jeff, who was doing well at Darlington Prep School in Rome, Georgia. He was making all A's and B's.

Prior to leaving, Marie, Ted, and Jeff joined me for some practice hiking in the Cumberland Mountains of Tennessee. Jeff related to me a lot of his experiences on his Outward Bound trip in Colorado the past summer. He told me how he dealt with the high altitudes, snow, cold, and sometimes miserable conditions. I remembered him saying, "Dad, this is really going to be hard for you. I don't know if you can make it or not." I thought about him so much and now had a new appreciation for him, knowing what he had gone through on that outward-bound experience.

Contrary to the previous night, I no longer had fear. My mental attitude was 180 degrees from the night before. About 2:00 a.m., I decided it best to relieve myself under the beauty of the heavens instead of in my sleeping bag. It was freezing cold, but like the night before, I was amazed to see so many stars. The smoke from the porters' campfire curled upward into the crystal-clear sky. The only sounds came from a dog barking in the distance. The feeling enveloped me that all signs were "go," and I was now ready to press on to that hallowed mountain called Everest.

DAY 3

By 5:30 a.m., I was ready to get out of that sleeping bag. I decided to go for a walk. Dawn is always a very special time. No matter which way I turned, I could see those beautiful Himalayas in every direction. The word Hima means snow, and Alaya means home. The name certainly fits because blankets of snow have found a home in these mountains, and the soft glow of sunrise is something to behold.

I returned to the tent; George was getting up. We took a walk together. As a geologist, he had a special knowledge and interest about rock formations and the history of the Himalayas. They are relatively new mountains, geologically speaking, and are continuing to grow at a rather rapid rate of an inch or so each year. George explained that the Indian plate is pressing up against the Asian plate, forcing these mountains in the middle to grow in height.

We watched older men walking alone, chanting or saying their mantra. The Buddhist chant, prayer, or mantra is *Om Mani Padme Hum*, which is written on all the prayer walls, prayer wheels, and chanted by all good Buddhists. Of course, it is written in Tibetan script.

Our usual breakfast of oatmeal, eggs, toast, and tea tasted good after a brisk morning walk. I decided to spice it up with some of my mixture from home, made from bran, wheat germ, lecithin, and brewer's yeast. I couldn't believe it when Pema pulled out a plastic jar of peanut butter. The label said it was made in Calcutta. It was dry and hard with a faint taste of peanut butter — definitely not as good as Jiffy Extra Crunchy.

This day's hike up to Namche Bazaar was supposed to be our most difficult thus far. Some of the trail had been washed out, and the detour required some steep climbing. We would be going from Monjo located at 9,500 feet to Namche at 11,500 feet. The weather was perfect for hiking. It was cold and clear as a bell. The temperature was slightly above freezing, although there were patches of ice. My excitement was building because the day had come when we would get our first glimpse of Mount Everest. That was what had brought me 15,000 miles from home. I wanted to gaze at the highest mountain peak in the world.

The trail headed down to the river. We passed through thickets of rhododendrons. For the first time, we saw bamboo on the mountainside and hiked through large patches of it. I certainly didn't know that bamboo grew at such a high altitude.

The detour caused us to do a lot of up-and-down

climbing. In some places, it seemed to be downright dangerous. The trail narrowed at some points where it was only wide enough to fit the width of one shoe. When you looked down and saw how far you would fall if you made a misstep, you realized that this place was not for the faint-hearted.

Hikers were going in both directions. We were told that a few years earlier you never saw another hiker. Now, there were many Americans, British, French, Germans, and Australians.

After negotiating that torturous detour, we crossed the river and started our straight-up ascent to Namche Bazaar. This climb was a real killer. I made up my mind that I didn't care if it took me all day. I was not going to rush. It's fun to casually walk and take pictures.

I brought along some powdered Gatorade for mixing in my canteen of water. It always helps to have a little extra spurt of energy. Marie had made gorp, consisting of peanuts, raisins, and M&M's. I brought honey candy from the health food store, so I had all of the ingredients to give me that extra boost when I sorely needed it.

We finally arrived at the point on the trail where we rounded a curve and beheld Mount Everest, towering in all of its majesty and glory off in the distance. It gave me cold chills. Just seeing it made me want to continue on, to get closer to it. Mount Lhotse was visible to the right of Everest, and Nuptse to the left of it. What a thrill to be in these magnificent surroundings!

Our trail was an ancient one, thousands of years old. The traders from India used to come to Namche, bringing their grains to exchange with the Tibetans for salt. Thus, Namche acquired its name as a bazaar for trading. The town is thousands of years old and is situated in a bowl surrounded by those beautiful snowcapped mountains.

We entered the Sagarmatha National Park where we presented our trekking permits and paid a fee. They handed us a brochure, and the very first sentence in the brochure stated, "One out of every one thousand people who enter this park will die of altitude sickness," a rather sobering thought which nagged somewhere in the back of my mind.

If one gets altitude sickness, there is nothing to do except go down to the lowest altitude you can find, and, generally, the symptoms go away. The bad thing was that there was no communication to the outside world except radio equipment at the airport in Lukla and a radio in Namche Bazaar. There they could call a helicopter in Katmandu but only in extreme cases and only if you had $1,500 in cash or an insurance policy which could be purchased in Katmandu. The other problem was that the helicopter could only fly in clear weather because it had no instruments.

In our orientation, we had been told not to give any candy or sweets to the Sherpa children along the trail because there were no dentists. Apparently, the advent of the trekkers brought new problems for the Sherpas. These new visitors were giving candy and chewing gum to the little kids, and for the first time in the history of their civilization, they were experiencing tooth decay.

The other admonition we'd been given was no cutting or burning wood. Apparently, over the past years, the mountains had been denuded of trees and there had been no replanting. Every group entering the Sagarmatha National Park was required to carry kerosene or some type of fuel for cooking. There seemed to me to be plenty of trees along the river here, and most all of the trees in this section were blue Himalayan pine.

The trail up to Namche was like climbing several miles of stairsteps into the heavens, reminiscent of my hike from the Colorado River up to the South Rim of the Grand Canyon. Only then, I had a 50-pound pack. My handicap on this ascent was the altitude. The leather Danner hiking boots I had purchased a few months previously were getting broken in on this hike.

The Gatorade and honey candy seemed to be wearing out, so I broke into song. There was no one in sight to hear me, I thought, and I gave one of my most soulful renditions of "Amazing Grace."

I didn't realize that Lhakpa was sitting on a rock above the trail, listening to my mournful plea.

Trudging around a curve, I saw him sitting there in view. He tried to drown me out with the only American song he knew, "Oh, my darling, oh, my darling, oh, my darling Clementine."

We had a good laugh.

Namche Bazaar is in the center of the Khumbu region and the only village other than Lukla that has any shops. Every Saturday people from all over the region go there to trade their goods and wares. Very few, if any of them, have money, but they barter in order to get their goods. The government of Nepal does not provide any funds for the poor. They have no medical aid or food stamps. The people still live and interact in the same manner that they did a thousand years ago. I guess there was really no necessity to have much money because there was very little to buy. However, the Sherpas were considered by the rest of the Nepalese to be the wealthiest people in Nepal.

The reason for this, of course, was because the trekking parties up to Mount Everest in the previous ten years had brought money into the region. Although these porters and guides were only paid two or three dollars a day, that was big money for them. All of the small children had as their life's ambition to be a porter and/or guide when they grew up.

The Sirdars were well-respected among the rest of the Sherpas and considered to be rather wealthy. The only thing I saw that they had which the others did not have was maybe a wool sweater, a wool cap, and some hiking shoes in the tennis or running shoe variety. Sometimes they were able to get a backpack because a lot of the Everest expeditions discarded all of their equipment afterwards and distributed it to their Sherpa guides and porters.

In Namche Bazaar, we pitched our tents in a yak yard enclosed by a stone wall in the back of the Kala Pattar Hotel. Don't be fooled by the word "hotel." It was a two-story stone structure with one dormitory room about 15 x 30 feet. A wooden platform had been built about three feet off the floor on both sides of the room with two-inch foam cushions all placed side-by-side. It was not a Hilton.

I sat in my tent inside my sleeping bag because after the sun goes down behind the mountains at around 2:00 p.m., the temperature started dropping dramatically. I had my tent flap open and watched a woman picking up fresh yak dung. She placed it in a metal bowl and then brought it over to the stone wall. With her hands, she patted it into a large pancake and slapped it up on the side of the wall. The entire wall was covered with these yak dung pancakes. The Sherpas used this for starting their fires. Inside the houses, they kept a stack of them next to the fireplace and occasionally would throw one on to start the fire burning.

While I was sitting there, writing in my journal, I was startled out of my wits by a yak who stuck his head through my tent flaps to see if I had anything he wanted. Fortunately, he didn't see anything of interest and walked away.

We had ascended 2,000 feet in altitude since Monjo. Namche Bazaar is 11,500 feet. As I lay in my tent, I began to feel a little nausea. Lhakpa tapped on my tent and summoned me for dinner. Food didn't sound very appetizing because I was feeling like it wouldn't take much effort for me to throw up. I sat there inside the hotel watching George and Mary attempt to eat. It was an effort to carry on a conversation with them.

George was still suffering from diarrhea and seemed to be growing weaker. He had begun to take Lomotil, but without much relief. Mary was feeling dizzy so most of our conversation centered around our ailments.

At one point, I interrupted their eating to ask Mary to hand me the empty bowl on the floor. I was beginning to feel like the heaving was about to start but nothing happened. There was a sensation of being seasick in a boat out in the ocean with no way to get off. My head was hurting and all of a sudden I began to shake all over. The shivering and shaking would not stop. These are classic signs of altitude sickness.

Mary ran off to get Mailapemba. It was dark and snowing outside. I kept remembering those words from the book that if you get the symptoms, you must descend immediately. The people who die are those who ignore the warnings and don't descend.

Mailapemba brought in the medical kit and pulled out his instruction book. He obviously couldn't read a word of English so he handed it to George to read aloud. My anxiety attacks were bordering on panic. With a wife and three children, I didn't want to become one of those one-in-a-thousand statistics.

Mailapemba pulled out a small cylinder of oxygen which none of us knew he had. He placed the mask over my face and turned it on. I started breathing deeply. It was absolutely amazing. Within a minute, I began to feel relief. The nausea disappeared, the headache subsided, and the shaking stopped. In his calm, bedside manner, Mailapemba began to speak of his experiences on Mount Everest, Annapurna, Ama Dablang, and others with German, Australian, and Austrian teams. He said that many of the climbers get sick and have to go back down. I couldn't believe that after using the oxygen for about five minutes, I really felt fine. It was amazing.

Mailapemba sent Pema and Lhakpa down to the tent to bring my sleeping bag and personal gear up to the indoor sleeping quarters. He said it was extremely important for me to stay warm and even though there was no heat inside, it would be warmer than the tent. Of course, it was not more than a couple of degrees warmer than outside, but that cold, icy ground does penetrate through a sleeping pad. I felt quite happy to stay inside.

I didn't sleep a wink all night. It must have been the longest night of my life. My throat was so sore I could hardly swallow. I decided that it would be best for me to head back down the mountain the next morning.

A 2,000-foot descent should cure my problems.

I thought about hiring a porter to take me back to Lukla and wait the necessary days to fly back to Katmandu. Maybe I would just try to find another trek besides this one where you didn't climb to such high altitudes. President Carter had told me how much he enjoyed the Chitwan National Forest and the elephant ride to Tiger Tops down in the southern part of Nepal.

That settles it, I thought. I'll do that at sun-up.

To make matters worse, those Hindus marched around town during the night singing at the top of their voices, playing tambourines, and celebrating the New Year. The monotony of their singing was enough to drive a man crazy. There must have been 100 dogs in Namche that barked all night long. What a miserable night!

DAY 4

Dawn came about 5:30 a.m. I felt hungry, but still had a slight headache. Mailapemba, who had slept next to me all night, told me to take an aspirin and stay in the sleeping bag. I first argued about the aspirin. I told him that I didn't like to take drugs. He insisted. At this point, I would have done anything he asked. He had nurtured me through the night with his kindness, so I took the aspirin. It was amazing how much better I felt, and what was even more astounding was the difference in the way I felt in the daytime versus the night. Those Himalayan nights would bring out all my worst fears and anxieties.

After eating a hearty breakfast, Mailapemba told me to take a walk around the town to see how I felt. He assured me that if I felt bad, he would send someone down with me. We could camp by the river until I felt better. George also complained to Mailapemba about his bad diarrhea and growing weaker. Mary had a headache and felt light-headed and giddy. We all sat around looking at each other and discussing our miseries.

"How could anyone think that this is fun?" George groaned. "I wish I had gone on a cruise to Fiji."

Mary agreed. "I was thinking of some of those beautiful beaches in Southern India."

Mailapemba encouraged me to walk up to the top of the hill where there was a national park office. It was about 600 feet straight up from Namche Bazaar. There, you could get a panoramic view of Mount Everest, Lhotse, Ama Dablang, and all the big ones.

I started walking down the cobbled streets watching other trekkers. The herdsmen were packing up their yaks with trekking equipment. Namche was the point where we had to drop the porters who had no shoes. They returned to Lukla to hire out to more hikers. Because of the ice, snow, and much colder weather higher up, it was best to use yaks.

Walking was not easy because I seemed weak. Each time I walked two steps, I had to stop and rest. That seemed to answer my dilemma which made me sad. I would not be able to go any higher. It was a shame to have to turn back.

I sat down feeling that I was in a quandary. I had only viewed such a small glimpse of Everest and had come all that distance not to mention the money, the year of training, and so many other things. I made up my mind to try to walk up that hill to the national park office, take some pictures of the mountains, and then go back down to the river that afternoon. It was a beautiful, clear day, although very cold. It could not have been a more perfect time for taking photos. If I could just photograph Everest from the top of that hill, I knew I would be satisfied. It wouldn't feel so bad having to turn back.

The walk was really straight up and didn't offer much assistance to the weary. It was icy and difficult walking. I kept pushing forward knowing somehow that God would give me the strength to make it. I looked up and out of nowhere appeared Mailapemba with his smiling Sherpa face showing all of his teeth. He seemed so wise. I sometimes felt that he could look at me and read all my thoughts. His brother was a Buddhist monk in a monastery in Katmandu, and Mailapemba also practiced the Buddhist attitude toward life. They seemed to be so happy-go-lucky, and nothing in the world bothered them.

He reached out. "Let me carry your pack," he offered.

I resisted because it was only a daypack with my camera and some personal items. "It probably doesn't weigh more than ten pounds," I insisted.

He looked at me with those all-knowing eyes.

At this point, I guess I would have done anything in the world he asked me to do. I tore off my last bit of male ego and handed him my pack. It did lighten the load.

Instead of resting every two steps, I only had to rest after every five steps.

He was so patient and didn't mind at all. Whatever I said or whatever I wanted to do was fine with him. We reached the top of the hill, and there it was. What an incredible view!

There wasn't a single cloud in the sky. It was worth the whole trip. You could see the Tengboche Monastery about halfway between where we were standing and Mount Everest. I took picture after picture, hoping to capture the feeling. It was such a beautiful sight. I could sense my spirits rising; I felt much better. We looked in each other's eyes, and somehow I could feel his spirit saying to me, "You must go on."

Mailapemba had George and Mary's trekking permits, and we were obliged to go to the national park office to register. Everyone who goes on from this point must sign in there. The attendant in the office asked me to read the notice board. I did, and there were some ten to fifteen notes pinned to the board relating to missing persons with messages like: IF ANYONE HAS SEEN JOE JONES AND JOHN SMITH FROM TORONTO, CANADA, PLEASE LET US KNOW. THEY LEFT FROM HERE ON OCTOBER 15 AND HAVE NOT BEEN SEEN OR HEARD FROM SINCE. Hikers were supposed to inform this national park office of their expected date of return, and they put notices up for the long-overdue trekkers.

Here was another sobering thought that lingered in my mind about how dangerous this trip was. I told Mailapemba, "Look, Man, I've got a wife and three children at home, and if I keep going up, you've got to promise me that you will get me back down safely."

He smiled.

I felt like I could read his thoughts. As any good Buddhist would say, "It is not up to you and me; it is up to God."

By this time, I had so much confidence in this man, I would have let him take me anywhere. I was happy that I had not undertaken this trip alone.

The Sherpas are such wonderful people, so friendly and helpful. As Buddhists, they believe you must do your best at what you do, regardless of benefit, because the benefits will be your karmic reward. They are so totally trustworthy. Even though the Sherpas have no formal education, they seem so knowledgeable and wise about life. Most of them not only speak their native Sherpa language but also speak Nepalese, some English and Tibetan. The Sherpa language is very similar to Tibetan, and the Nepalese language is similar to the northern Indian dialects. It had become very clear to me why western mountain climbers trust these Sherpa guides with their lives.

When I returned to the teahouse in Namche, I was convinced that the only decision was to keep on going. My only malady at the time was a sore throat and some sinus congestion. That seemed to be chronic with all the trekkers who had come back down from the higher altitudes with terrible coughs, colds, sniffing, sneezing, etc. The place where I slept advertised hot showers. I was tempted. For 15 rupees, I could find out what it was like.

It was a small closet area about 3 feet by 3 feet outside. Hot water, which had been heated over the fire, was placed in a container above. When the string was pulled, the water came out through a hole. I pulled off those clothes I had been wearing since Katmandu and removed one layer of dust and dirt from my body. It really felt good. I had assumed in the beginning of the trip that we would be able to bathe in the streams as we went along. It was apparent that that would never take place.

For one thing, the rivers are freezing cold due to melted glaciers and snow. Second, the custom of the Sherpas is that they should never expose their nude bodies to another. In our briefing, they warned us of this and discouraged violating their customs. It is even considered lewd for women to wear pants or skirts above their ankles. The local women wear long dresses made of very thick material that almost drag the ground. They usually have some kind of sweater for warmth. We were told that a man must never show any kind of affection for a woman in public, even if she is his wife. If he were to hold her hand or touch her in any way in the presence of others, this would indicate that she was a very loose, lewd woman.

DAY 5

Dawn arrived in Namche after a much more pleasant night. You have to make a decision old boy, I said to myself. Do you want to keep going up or go back down?

I no longer had any symptoms of altitude sickness, only a head cold. My nose was running, sneezing, and I had a sore throat.

The sun peeped over the mountains. The day was bright and clear. With weather that beautiful, there was no doubt I had to keep trudging on.

From Namche Bazaar, we walked along a ridge, above the tree line, for a couple of hours, then made a descent straight down to the river. The scenery was spectacular with picturesque views of Everest, Ama Dablang, and the rest of those giants towering above the trail in all of their splendor. We now had three yaks carrying our supplies. But, thank goodness, we had Mailapemba, Pema, and Lhakpa as our guides and cooks. The two sisters were still with us assisting with the cooking and cleaning.

We occasionally met other trekkers both ascending and descending. I liked to have a little conversation with everybody I met along the trail. It was interesting to find out where they were from and to hear their most profound experiences of the past few days. One couple going in our same direction asked me where I was from.

When I told them, the girl said, "Well, I have been to St. Simons Island and visited Eric Kocher. Do you know him?"

I told her that he was a good friend of mine and was practicing law in Atlanta.

She and her husband lived in Hong Kong, but she was originally from Jacksonville, Florida. She said her parents had western-and-jeans stores called Sagara's in the Regency and Orange Park Malls. It seemed funny to be halfway around the world and meet somebody who had lived one hour from my home.

It was fun going downhill, but the only bad thing is that eventually you have to pay. When we reached the river, it meant straight up the mountainside to Tengboche.

As our trekking party moved along, I had some time to spend walking alone. I always liked that. It gave me the time to soak up the beauty of the surroundings and enjoy it to the fullest. I tried constantly to keep my mind in the present, observing all of the little things like birds and small flowers popping out of the ground that seemed so out of place. When one pays close attention to the present, great pleasure can be found in the awareness of small things. I had decided that I was there only to be there. I resigned myself to the fact that I should have no destination. If I could make it up to Everest Base Camp, Kala Pattar, or wherever, that would be fine. If I didn't, that would be fine, too. I had seen beautiful sights and was becoming much more aware of all of the surroundings. It was enjoyable being alone, nary a sound could be heard. It was deathly quiet.

No airplanes ever flew near the Himalayas to etch any streaks in the cloudless skies or to make noises. The only sounds that I could hear were my boots trudging along that rocky trial. I wore no watch. Time had no meaning.

Occasionally, there were Buddhist prayer flags on poles and houses, and I respected their traditions by keeping them always on my right side. One old man who passed by held his prayer beads and chanted as he walked along, "*Om Mani Padme Hum.*"

I was beginning to realize that I had absolutely no communication with the outside world but total communication with the Earth. Crossing the river on the little foot bridge, I came upon a teahouse. I sat beside the water with numerous prayer wheels being turned by the current to send the Buddhist chant in all directions according to their beliefs. After I crossed the water, I recognized the familiar faces of George and Mary and all of my Sherpa gang sitting around waiting for me to arrive. George and Mary were having tea, and I quickly joined them. We had dropped almost 2,000 feet from Namche Bazaar to this place named Pungo Tenga. It was very pretty beside the river, and I liked listening to the flowing water. All of my bodily functions, especially my mind, had slowed down to a snail's pace. I especially enjoyed being alone and decided to tell the rest of the party to go ahead and make their afternoon ascent up to Tengboche without me.

I cleared it with Mailapemba to be sure I could stay in the little teahouse for the night. I promised to make that steep climb up to the Tengboche Monastery the next morning. He wanted to give me some drugs from the first-aid kit to doctor my sinuses and runny nose. He was trying to look out for me, but I knew that he wouldn't take them himself. It took a while to convince him that I would take lots of vitamin C, drink plenty of water, and get a good night's sleep. That was better than drugs.

Mary commented that this high-altitude thing felt to her like a case of the flu, and no one wants to spend their vacation hiking in the mountains with a seasick stomach and a pounding head. The three of us agreed that anyone in his right mind would turn around and go back. But who wanted to wait one week in Lukla for a flight back to Katmandu. We were there, like it or not. The scenery was by far the most spectacular that any of us had seen in our lifetimes, but all of us had a nagging uneasiness that if we wanted or needed to get out in a hurry, we could not.

We bid our goodbyes and they started their upward climb. It was hard to conceal my happiness watching them march off in single fashion followed by three huge yaks. I found that my mind was much more at ease when I didn't have to listen to their aches and pains. I could see the Sherpas walking up the narrow pathway with the yak man and trailing along behind. When you hire yaks to carry the baggage, the owner of the yaks must come along with them.

I honestly could not see how those yaks were able to negotiate the trail. There were some places where it was so narrow that one misstep would be a drop one mile down into the river or a ravine. I wondered how many yaks might have fallen. It was always disconcerting when I was on the trail and met a group of yaks coming my way. I had to press my body up against the mountainside of the trail and let them have the outside.

I spent the entire afternoon sitting on a rock overlooking the rushing mountain stream. The noise was deafening but also hypnotic. I do love nature and enjoy it most while hiking in the mountains. My only regret on this trip was that I had never hiked anywhere before without feeling very good and exhilarated. It does take some of the charm away when you don't feel your best.

The previous night at Namche, I had walked over to the western part of the village to watch the sun setting on the snowcapped mountains. It was such a gorgeous sight to see. A fellow from Australia came up and started talking to me. This was his second time in the Himalayas, and he loved it. He was on his way back down, having been up to Gorek Shep where he stayed one night. He said the temperature up there was minus 22 degrees (F.). For us, the weather everyday had been perfect. In the middle of the day, it warmed up into the 30's with bright sunshine. It was ideal weather for walking. This was a once-in-a-lifetime trip that I would probably never do again. The spectacular views I had seen were worth all of the pain and suffering.

That evening at Pungo Tenga was a time for me to work on getting my body back into good physical shape. George had left me some of his throat lozenges, and I needed something to get rid of my stuffy head and runny nose.

The little room in the teahouse slept nine people. One young fellow from New York had come down with bad headaches higher up at Dengboche and had to come down to lower altitudes. Two Australians, one an older man, became sick in their party and didn't feel like going any higher. A San Francisco man tried to reach Island Peak, which requires some amount of technical climbing, and he had gotten sick. So, I felt like I was sleeping in a sick ward. People were coughing and really hacking, trying to get the fluid out of their lungs.

The family who ran the teahouse was interesting. A little ten-year-old girl worked very hard at satisfying everyone's requests for food and tea while her mother, father, and old grandmother sat around the kitchen next to the fire.

Custom requires that you must remove your shoes before entering into a Buddhist home. It is impolite to ever touch anything inside a house with your shoes. Also, you should never point your feet toward any sacred thing, the fireplace, or in the direction of people. It also violates custom to shake hands with them or touch them in any way. You should only greet them and bid them goodbye by saying, "*Namaste.*"

For supper, they served lots of potatoes, cabbage, and a pot full of noodles. An Australian man next to me ordered potatoes, and the little girl brought him about 15 potatoes in a bowl, each the size of a large lemon. He looked at that mound of potatoes and started laughing. He said there was no way in the world he could eat that much. "Can somebody help me?" he moaned.

I ordered noodles and cabbage, but they stirred them in a frying pan with some kind of oil that made it so greasy, it was not very palatable. I tried very hard to eat it because she prepared it especially for me, but I just couldn't stomach that much grease. All of us drank heartily of yak milk tea. They heat the milk to a boil, then add loose tea leaves to the milk. Sugar is mixed with it and served piping hot in a glass. It really hit the spot on such a cold night.

DAY 6

I woke early. The rest and relaxation were just what the doctor ordered. I felt anxious to get on with the program and start that climb up the mountain. My stomach wanted breakfast. The mother of the house had left for Namche about 6:00 a.m., and her little daughter was in charge. I couldn't help but think how my wife might handle a four-hour walk to the grocery store and four hours back. But you can't compare. Everything has a different perspective.

I sat with a French couple who had dropped in for eggs and pancakes. We had lots of time to talk. I must have waited about an hour before the little girl cooked and served me a bowl of porridge and milk tea. I felt sorry for her because she was overwhelmed with business.

Another in what seemed like an endless number of beautiful days had arrived, so I grabbed my trusty walking stick and headed straight up that mountain. Actually, I took it pretty easy, so it was almost three hours to make the ascent to Tengboche. The trail was a switchback; though the climb was strenuous, the scenery was breathtaking. I seemed to have overcome my maladies and was in good spirits when I arrived. I had a joyful reunion with all of my colleagues at Tengboche. We feasted on a hearty lunch of potatoes, egg salad, cabbage, and three slices of pineapple. My good appetite had returned.

The Tengboche Monastery was strategically placed on the highest point of this particular mountain, which is 13,000 feet in elevation. The building is pinkish-red in color and houses some 30 to 40 monks. It sits in the most outlandish and spectacular spot in the world. Never before had I experienced such exquisite beauty. In every direction, the towering Himalayas stood guard over this religious shrine.

I talked to Mailapemba and Pema about the possibility of meeting the Lama, the head priest of the monastery. Pema, who spoke the best English of all, went to the monastery to try to make arrangements for me to have an audience with him. I anxiously awaited Pema's return. He was gone for quite a while.

When he returned and told me that he had made an appointment for me to see the Lama, I got very excited. It was necessary to buy a ceremonial scarf to present to him. There was a nearby shop which coincidentally sells them. Actually, the scarf looked like a piece of cheese cloth. But at this point, I was not asking any questions — just going along for the trip.

Pema said that I must wrap a donation in the scarf when I presented it to him and that I should greet him, "*Namaskaar*." It is the more polite and formal version of *Namaste*, but still means "I behold the God within you."

We entered the monastery, and then into a small room (approximately 15 feet by 15 feet) which was some type of anteroom. Two of its sides had windows with stunning views. The south side overlooked the mountain of Chambu-Ila, and the north side looked smack into the south face of Chomolungma (Mount Everest). We were sitting in the back of the room when the door opened.

The Lama entered with his long, flowing maroon robe and shaved head. I was in awe of this holy man but remembered to put my hands together in prayer-like fashion and to greet him with my most polite, "*Namaskaar*." I dutifully stretched out my hands holding the scarf and a 20-rupee bill wrapped in it.

He broke the silence with a very warm, "*Namaskaar*." He blessed me as he took the scarf and draped it around my neck. He began speaking to Pema and me in a very soft-spoken Tibetan language.

Pema, who of course spoke Tibetan fluently, would occasionally stop and interpret what he was saying. To begin with, it was mostly small talk.

One of the Lama's aides entered with a tray of cups filled with Tibetan tea. They drink their tea with butter and salt, which I presume must be an acquired taste.

I showed him my blue book, *The Quiet Mind*, which I take with me wherever I go. It contains hundreds of prayers. I told him that I keep it in my pocket when hiking and ever so often, when I find an appropriate rock or resting spot, I read it for inspiration.

He responded approvingly, saying that was very good.

I told him that I meditated daily.

He nodded affirmatively, as if I had said that I also breathe.

The Lama and Pema talked incessantly, and I wanted so much to know what they were saying. It may have been impolite, but I walked to the back of the room where I had spotted a map of the world. I interrupted them to show them where in America I lived and the route I took to get from my home to Nepal. He told me that he had also traveled. I asked him where, and he responded, "To Tibet." He had visited a monastery in Lhasa, the capital city. I didn't know how far that was, but it was across the Himalayas. It must have been about 50 miles from Tengboche.

I asked him about the Dalai Lama, the head

Lama of all Buddhism. When the Communists took over Tibet in the late 1950s and early 1960s, he escaped and had been living in exile in the northwest of India.

He had met the Dalai Lama when he was a young boy, which must be, for a Buddhist, like meeting God. It was impossible to enter Tibet without a special visa that was difficult to get. The Nepalese government had arranged the trip for him. He told of staying in various monasteries along the way. The building in Tengboche is relatively new, having been built in 1915. The young boys in the Khumbu region are chosen to be monks when they are about ten years old. It is considered a great honor for the family if their son is taken away to live in this monastery for the rest of his life.

In an effort to prolong the conversation, I asked him how long he had been the Lama at Tengboche. "Since the fourteenth century," was Pema's interpretation of his answer. I was a bit taken aback by his answer and thought that Pema had made a mistake. But then I remembered the Buddhist's staunch belief in reincarnation. Pema later explained that when the Lama sheds this earthly body, his spirit returns very soon to inhabit another one. It is up to the monks of the monastery to search him out. They take some of the Lama's personal items to all the newborn males in the area. The one who makes the appropriate identification is declared to be the reincarnated Lama.

The Lama gazed out the window at Chambu-Ila and began talking about the spirituality of the Himalayan mountains. I sincerely believed him. There was certainly something of a higher nature that one could feel in those surroundings. After a visit of about 30 minutes, the conversation had run its course. We stood up and bid a reverent *"Namaskaar"* to each other.

Pema then escorted me into the monastery itself to the main sanctuary. We removed our shoes and went inside. A large Buddha sat at the far end, and colorful rugs hung from the rafters. Rolled up prayer scrolls had been placed in slots all around the room. Candles were lighted everywhere. Six monks sat on one side of the room and six on the other with their floor-length maroon robes wrapped around them. All had shaved heads. They were chanting and playing musical instruments, a very large drum, cymbals, small horns, two large Alpine horns, and even some smaller bongo-like drums. The sounds were weird and not very melodic. The whole thing gave me an eerie feeling.

At various points, they would stop the music and start chanting again. One monk would go around with a large kettle and pour some type of liquid in a small metal cup in front of each monk. The floor, made of stone, was extremely cold. It was colder inside than outside, which was in the 30's.

A native worshiper but not a monk came in the door and sat down in the back of the sanctuary. One of the monks went over and gave him a cup of steeping hot tea in a china cup. I wished so much for some of it, but I didn't rate. I was doing my best to take everything in. One monk was sound asleep in the back. At first I thought he was mediatating until I heard him snoring.

The cold from the stone floor was beginning to penetrate into my body. The heavy wraps worn by the monks seemed to be thick and warm. I supposed they were accustomed to the cold, but I was not. I wanted to stay longer to observe this strange ceremony, and even more so, I would like to have taken pictures, but that was strictly prohibited. This whole trip had been such a great experience. Everything I saw was all so different and unusual.

When the sun started dropping behind the mountain, the temperature plummeted. I wanted to watch the sun set on Everest, but it was much too cold to stay outside. Inside the local teahouse, I found a window to observe this beautiful sight for the first time. It was so pretty to see the colors on the snow changing first from a cream color to a yellow to a pinkish hue, then reddish, then maroon, and finally black. Watching this sunset was worth the whole trip. I sat in that window for about an hour and took loads of pictures. But I knew there was no way that a photo could let anyone know how it really felt to be there and observe it firsthand.

I had to decide whether to sleep in the tent with George or sleep inside the teahouse. Mary was sleeping inside; although the teahouse had no heat, it was still warmer than the tent. The teahouse consisted of three rooms composed of a kitchen and two sleeping rooms. Since the kitchen was separated from the other rooms, the sleeping portion was not so smoky. Eight people were on each side of the room, all sleeping side by side.

No matter how good I felt in the daytime, darkness always brought about an unsettling feeling. I don't know why, but the others sensed the same thing. All of the booger bears came out at night. At some point, Mary woke me out of a deep sleep saying that she was ill. I felt her forehead, and she was perspiring. Since it was below freezing inside, I knew she must really be sick. She felt nauseous.

I jumped out of my bag and found a cooking pot

in the kitchen. There was no light so I had to feel my way around. I returned just in time for her to start throwing up in it.

Three girls from Seattle, all nurses, slept just across from us. One came over to give aid. Mary was very afraid. I knew how she felt. When you are in this situation, you don't know if you are dying of altitude sickness or not. I summoned Mailapemba, Lhakpa, and Pema from their tent.

In the back of all of our minds was the warning that this is not something to mess around with. It is fatal, and the only sure cure is to descend immediately. The question we were facing was whether to descend in the middle of a subzero night or wait until morning.

Pema got out the medicine kit with the little oxygen tank that had brought me back to life. I found a thermometer and took her temperature. It read in centigrade, so I didn't know if 37 degrees was normal or not. A German trekker raised up in his bed and reckoned that it was about 100 degrees Fahrenheit. Mary was very nauseated and had a splitting headache. We gave her oxygen but it was no help. She didn't want to take any medicine and decided to try to tough it out until morning. Everyone else went back to bed. All night long, she threw up. I sat in my sleeping bag beside her. Neither of us slept one wink the entire night.

DAY 7

Dawn came about 5:30 a.m. I felt Mary's forehead. She was still hot and her breathing was very heavy. I could see Mount Everest out of the window. I stayed in my warm sleeping bag and watched the sunrise put on a light show. At first, it illuminated the peak of snow on the top of Everest and then gradually the light unveiled the whole mountain. It was too spectacular for words, although I must admit the sunset was prettier because the colors and glows were softer.

Tengboche had such magnificent views that I didn't care if I went any farther or not. It suited me to stay there the entire time and enjoy the beautiful scenery.

All the people I met were coughing, sniffing, sneezing, and telling me of their vomiting, diarrhea, and you name it.

Is this the craziest thing I have ever done in my life? I wondered.

It seemed stupid to see these people harming their health just to see some mountains. However, somehow there was a magnetic pull and tugging that made people keep going on. We were only at 13,000 feet, but it was definitely not easy getting there. I had made it that far strictly by the grace of God and a lot of praying. It had been a great deal more difficult and physically demanding than I ever realized.

Mary was feeling rotten. George had diarrhea so bad that he had to get up four times during the night, but he was still hell-bent on continuing. I felt fine, but since I had not slept during the night, I didn't feel that I was ready for a six-hour hike up to Dengboche.

You could hear the loud cymbals clashing, bells

ringing, and horns blowing at the monastery. It had been going on since before dawn. Supposedly, it occurred every single day of their lives. I couldn't decide whether I envied them for living in this most beautiful spot in the world or pitied them for never being able to leave.

The three of us split up that morning. George took off for Dengboche with the three nurses from Seattle. Mary went back down the mountain to Pungo Tenga with Lhakpa, and I wanted to have my day of rest there at Tengboche. Poor Mailapemba had to deal with three people all going in different directions. However, in typical, easy-going, Sherpa fashion, it didn't seem to bother him a bit. He worked right through it without getting upset. The Sherpas must be the most laid-back, helpful, and loving people in the world, I thought. They were always right there "johnny on the spot."

I was quite happy just to laze around and enjoy the beauty. I met a woman from California. Her husband was the doctor in charge of one of the Mountain Travel Tours from Albany, California. They had a group of about twenty people who were there for six weeks. She told me about their adventures and said that many of them were sick. She had left the group and decided to come back down to Tengboche. She said that this place felt like a Bahamian Island compared to those freezing temperatures up higher in the mountains. She and her husband had hiked all over the world. They had four children, two boys (24 and 23) and two girls (21 and 19). We talked quite a long time, while basking out in the sun, about our children, about mountain hiking, and things in general.

The outdoor privy at Tengboche was the most

unusual one I had ever experienced. It literally over-hung the side of the mountain. An unnerving feeling overcame me when I looked through the sitting hole and could see about 2,000 feet straight down. It had one good thing going for it. It was a completely odorless privy.

Toward the middle of the day, we watched a pitiful figure struggling back up the trail. It turned out to be George. He was walking like a dazed, drunk man. He said he had hiked as far as Pangboche but was so weak, he couldn't walk. That morning he had been so excited about going with the three nurses, but now he seemed like a broken old man, very depressed.

Pema fixed lunch: a yak cheese sandwich, French fries, and a cup of *daal* (lentil) soup. It was delicious, and I enjoyed sitting out there in the open air in the sunshine.

After lunch, I walked off into the mountains. It was a pleasure to take photos of this beautiful place and also to have some quiet moments for meditation and reading. I came upon a yak or nak, as the case may be, grazing on the mountain side. A nak is a female. There was really not much to graze on because there was little or no plant life.

Large blackbirds were flying overhead. They landed near me and I could see that they were ravens. I reached in my sack of gorp, picked out the peanuts from the raisins and M&M's, and threw them on the ground. They flew right up within three or four feet of me. The birds looked at me and wondered what I was doing up there in their terri-tory. I wondered, too. Then, they flew off and cruised around. I envied them. I wondered if they appreci-ated living in the most beautiful and spectacular scenery in the world. It would be so nice to be able to fly around up there like a bird and go from one mountain to another. Is "a bird's eye view" anymore spectacular than a "man's eye view?"

When I returned to the camping area, new people were coming back down from the mountains. It was depressing talking with them because everyone had horror stories to tell about some terrible thing that had happened to them or someone else. One fellow from Scotland had been poisoned on honey that he and his friend ate in a teahouse. Most of the bees feed on the nectar from the rhododendron plants. Apparently, the rhododendrons are poisonous just like our oleanders in the South. He said that within an hour from the time they ate the honey, both of them were comatose on the floor and almost died.

They told stories of awful problems with altitude sickness. One older woman's legs were swollen to three or four times their normal size. She could not walk and had visited the clinic at Pheriche. Two sick Americans had paid the price to be helicoptered out. When the helicopter arrived to take them, she tried to get on, but they refused because her name was not on the list, and she had not paid in advance. Apparently, there was no way to be helicoptered out just because you may be sick. You must be dying and have the money to pay.

One of the trekkers told about one helicopter which had arrived at Lukla with 300 people on a waiting list. The pilot had room for 12 people. There were fights and shoving matches to see who could get on at $300 per person. Fifteen people jumped on, and they could not get three of them to leave. So, they called men to bodily remove the three, kicking and screaming. I recalled what that couple at Lukla told me when I got off the plane. "Get back on that plane. This is a trap."

On the trail to Mt. Everest

Tengboche Monastery — Ama Dablang in background.

Mount Everest and surroundings

Hostel in the forest, Brunswick, Georgia

Inside the teahouse, I found George crying in his bed. He tearfully told me about how he had trained for this trip all year long and wanted so badly to get to Kala Pattar. "Now," he said, "it's all over." He was too weak to walk because of the debilitating diarrhea.

It gave me guilt feelings; I was feeling in good condition. Obviously my body had acclimatized, at least to that particular level of 13,000 feet. After eating a hearty supper of good lentil soup, Sherpa stew over rice, and cake with jam and tea, I was totally relaxed. Not having had any sleep the night before, I hit the sack early. However, people were coming and going all night long in and out of the room.

As was usual, I had to get out of that warm sleeping bag about 1:30 a.m. to go outside in the freezing cold to urinate. I seemed to always wait until it became an emergency before getting out. However, after getting outside, it was worth it. There were billions of brilliant stars, maybe even three times as many as we see in North America. I gazed up at the heavens as long as I could stand the cold. The little dipper (Ursa Minor) was sitting right on top of Ama Dablang. What a picture! I wished for a tripod to get a shot of it.

DAY 8

George seemed to be feeling better and wanted to go with me up to Dengboche. We arose early, packed our duffel bags, and the Sherpas saddled up the yaks. It felt much colder. Ice covered the ground, but it was stimulating to me. In fact, I felt so exhilarated that I decided to take off ahead of everyone else. As usual, I always bundled up with too much clothes, and about ten minutes down the trail, I had to take some of them off. It seemed so hard for me to learn that once I started hiking, I was going to get very warm.

The trail followed level ground for a long time. It was such a nice day. Something hung down from the trees that looked like Spanish moss except it was thinner and wispier. After a while, we took a descent to the river for crossing. There were several people on the trail, and I always stopped them for a little conversation. After crossing the river, there was a great view of Ama Dablang. To me, it was the most beautiful of all the mountains. The Americans climbed to the summit in 1983. The name Ama Dablang means Grandmother's Locket.

Anytime that we crossed a river, it meant a more difficult task of ascending. The ascent led to Pangboche where I met up with George and the Sherpas for lunch.

The monastery in Pangboche claims to contain a Yeti's (abominable snowman) scalp. Naturally, there was argument about whether or not this was actually a Yeti scalp. Many scientists have studied Yeti patterns and have taken plaster-cast footprints of its wanderings in the vicinity of Mount Everest. There is no doubt that it is not like any human or animal we have ever known. Its feet are much too large. The older Sherpas had all heard tails of the Yeti, but the younger ones seemed to laugh it off as an old wives' tale.

Pema fixed a primo lunch with some hot vegetable soup, potatoes and slaw with tuna fish, and our usual three slices of pineapple. I commended him for bringing that can of tuna fish since it is one of my favorite things to eat.

In Pangboche, we saw old men and women digging potatoes out of the ground and piling them in large stacks. The young people put the potatoes in straw baskets for storing. This was their staple food and would last them through the winter.

After lunch, we continued to ascend. We were in excess of 15,000 feet, maybe even 16,000. While we were walking, Mailapemba and I stayed together and did a lot of talking. I began to feel light-headed, but didn't say anything about it. We kept plugging along. This dizziness made me feel a bit tipsy. I didn't want to stumble and hit my head on one of those rocks. The wind was blowing colder even though we were walking in the sun. I finally decided to tell Mailapemba about feeling a little drunk. He stayed right with me. It made me feel so much more secure. We passed by Ama Dablang. It was so beautiful that I continued to look back at it looming over my right shoulder.

We came to a fork in the trail. The left went to Pheriche and the right to Dengboche. Mailapemba said that Dengboche was not as cold as Pheriche because it was more protected from the wind. I dreaded to see the trail descending to the river again because it meant another ascent once we had crossed it. I had felt so exhilarated when I started that morning but later in the afternoon, as we reached higher altitudes, I was struggling along. George also walked very slowly, and both of us commented that it must be like being drunk or stoned. We headed toward Island Peak. At that point, Everest was hidden by Lhotse and the Nuptse Ridge.

We pitched our tents in a yak yard alongside a group of English trekkers who arrived before we did. This was to be our coldest night thus far. There was ice and snow on the ground. Mailapemba said that the temperature would be well below zero degrees Fahrenheit. We had to avoid hyperthermia. I felt giddy and completely disoriented. It seemed to take forever to arrange the items inside my tent.

While unpacking my duffel bag, I found myself picking up an item, just holding it, and looking at it. I couldn't make up my mind what to do with it. Looking back on it, I'm sure it was comical. Everything took much more of an effort, even taking off my boots.

One of the English campers had a small tape player. I laughed when I heard rock music being played way up there at the foot of Mount Everest. Many people were having difficulty pitching their tents on the ice and snow.

It was certainly worth the trip to see the most spectacular scenery in the world, but every person I met up there had some kind of malady. Some were more serious than others. It was like a group of escaped hospital patients all hacking, coughing, and throwing up as we proceeded higher and higher into the mountains. Was there some kind of magnetic power that kept all of us struggling toward some unknown goal, or were we all crazed lunatics?

I always hated to see nightfall come because whatever problem I might have would be magnified a hundred times. In fact, nights were absolutely miserable. You had to be in the sleeping bag at least by 7:00 p.m. or be frozen to death. The higher the altitude, the less you could sleep. So we spent about twelve hours going through every kind of death imaginable.

To avoid getting in the tent before sundown, I went into the little house next to the tent area where they were cooking the dinner. I had never felt like

that in my life. I kept thinking that if I closed my
eyes, I would pass out. People would try to talk to
me, but it was as if I was not there. I was floating
around somewhere. I had no headaches or nausea
but was feeling faint.

I sat there totally disoriented with about twelve
Sherpas around the fire. The room was completely
saturated with smoke. A young girl, who looked
about twelve, was nursing a baby she said was
twenty days old. The young-looking father sat beside
her. All of the others were sitting around drinking a
hot alcoholic drink they make from rice called
Chang. The stuff is thick and milky-looking and was
in the kettle over the fire. Whenever a Sherpa entered
the room, the woman of the house poured a glassful
to the rim and would not take "no" for an answer. If
he shook his head that he didn't want any, then she
not only gave it to him anyway but made him drink
it. Mailapemba told her that I could not have any
because I had to avoid altitude sickness. She respected his wishes and did not insist. I was glad but
couldn't have drunk it even if she made me.

The room was lighted by two candles and the
fire. I kept trying to breathe deeply so that I would
get as much oxygen as possible. The thick smoke
that blanketed the room didn't make it too palatable.
They were all carrying on a Sherpa conversation
while I sat around in outer space, not knowing what
was going on.

The dinner consisted of cauliflower, carrots,
creamed potatoes, and *daal* soup. I ate the soup and
drank some lemon tea but really didn't have much of
an appetite for eating anything else. I staggered out
to the tent. It was cold — really cold. I climbed inside
my sleeping bag that was only graded to minus 5

degrees (F.). I put on my wool socks, thermal bottoms, wool pants, thermal tops, wool sweater, down jacket, wool scarf, pulled my wool hat down over my head, and tightened the drawstring on my bag so that it left a hole about the size of a quarter next to my nose. It was unbelievable that I was still cold. Although when I remembered that I was actually sleeping on a block of ice, it was easier to understand. There was very little sleeping during the night because I never really did warm up. Occasionally I drifted in and out of sleep and had the weirdest dreams. I dreamed that I was a small child talking to many people who had been dead for years. I was a little boy again in Pineview, Georgia. It all seemed too abnormal and crazy.

DAY 9

One of the Sherpa girls tapped on the frozen tent about 7:00 a.m. with a cup of hot tea. I felt so rotten, like I had a bad hangover. Everything inside my tent was frozen. My water bottle was a block of ice, even my Dr. Bronner's liquid peppermint soap was frozen. When I crawled out of the tent to urinate, the ground was one solid block of ice. No chance of walking on it at all until the sun melted it slightly.

George and I spent some time discussing future plans. Should we go forward? Do we stay there? Do we go back down? George had this absolute obsession on making it all the way to Kala Pattar. I didn't have that same drive.

Mailapemba joined us in our tent to discuss our next move. George still felt horrible and had not recovered from his bad diarrhea. But he still wanted to try to climb higher. I told Mailapemba that I would like to stay there in Dengboche some additional time to attempt to acclimatize. He suggested that I might want to consider going back down since I was feeling so crazy the night before. He reckoned that even though I had no headaches and nausea or other typical altitude sickness symptoms, he had seen too many mountain climbers with the same symptoms of being disoriented that I had the previous night. He said that some of them became so confused and deranged that they couldn't even walk.

I respected his judgment. There was no particular reason to risk my life and limb to make some particular goal when I had already experienced the adventure of a lifetime and seen breathtaking, spectacular scenery. What else did I want to accomplish?

Mailapemba said that he would go with George up to Lobuche with one of the yaks. He left Pema and the other yak with me.

That suited me fine. Pema had become my good friend. He went to the little teahouse up the road to see if they had room for me to put my sleeping bag in there for the evening. The previous night was too cold on that icy ground. Even without heat, it would be a little warmer inside the teahouse.

Pema and I took all my necessary personal gear up there. Like all the others, there were about 12 to 15 spaces for sleeping on a wooden platform. A lot of the young hikers slept in teahouses because they carried all of their own gear and didn't hire any Sherpa porters or guides. That may be the cheapest way to make the trip, but I was quite satisfied having the Sherpas. In my estimation, they were invaluable with the information they gave us, not to speak of the lightened load.

I visited Dengboche's outdoor privy consisting of four stone walls with no roof. It only offers privacy

from people but not much shelter from the snow and
ice falling from the sky. Pema fixed the usual breakfast, and I was feeling fine. The sun came up bright
and clear. It looked as if it would be another beautiful day. I definitely wanted to do some hiking, so Pema
said he would take me to some of the surrounding
mountain peaks that would give excellent views of
Mount Everest. I appreciated his offer but told him I
would like to go alone. Anyway, he had already started
playing a game of craps with a couple of other Sherpas.
I knew he was just as happy to stay there.

The trail going up toward Lobuche was very icy.
As I ascended, it grew colder and colder. The wind
didn't help matters either. Dengboche was in a valley
probably around 15,000 feet. I started my ascent up
a slope approximately 16,500 feet. There's just not
much oxygen when you get up to that altitude. I saw
a couple of rock piles which appeared to be some
form of Buddhist monuments. I spotted a mountaintop with a steep trail leading up to it. It didn't
seem to have too much snow or ice. At first, I had to
take a few steps and then stop for a rest. Fortunately, I had the gorp and honey candy, which I kept
in my pocket. The Gatorade in my canteen also
helped to give me that extra boost of energy. I don't
know the name of this particular mountain, but it
sat next to and underneath Mount Everest. It is
probably what the Sherpas would call a hill, but for
me, it was a high mountain.

The higher I went, the more of a struggle it
became. I found that each time I put one foot down
in front of the other, it was necessary to stop for a
rest. I continued along with this exercise of putting
one more foot down and stopping to rest. It seemed
that it was going to take me forever, but something

inside kept telling me that I must reach the top. It did take a long time, but finally, I pulled my body up to the summit. It took every ounce of guts I had in me. When I got my wits about me, I stopped to look around. I was surrounded 360 degrees by the most beautiful snowcapped peaks of the spectacular Himalayas. I took out my camera and decided to make a shot in every direction. What an exhilarating experience! I felt so happy to be up there all alone viewing that gorgeous scenery. Surely heaven couldn't be any more beautiful!

I sat down to marvel at God's handiwork. I pulled out my blue book that I so often read for a word of inspiration. I thumbed the pages and randomly selected a passage. It seemed to jump out at me as I read:

> "It may comfort you to know that every one of you who undergoes some experience involving pain and anguish, and which might be described as a crucifixion, is doing something for the whole world. For anyone who meets such testings of the soul in the same resolute and tranquil spirit (in however small degree) as did the Master Jesus, is helping to quicken the vibrations of the whole earth."

As I read these words, I began to cry. I cried and cried and cried as if my whole insides were coming out. I knew for the first time why I had to do this and why I had to go up on that mountaintop alone. As Jesus, Moses, and many others had encountered spiritual experiences on a mountaintop, I knew, too, that God was speaking to me to renew my faith. It was necessary to humble myself in the midst of His mastery. I thanked God over and over for allowing me such an experience and pledged my life and soul to God for the rest of my days.

It was the most awe-inspiring experience of my life. I felt renewed. I felt fulfilled. I knew now why I had come. Why I had endured pain and suffering. I now felt whole. I felt content, without any fear or anxiety.

I stayed up there as long as I could stand the cold. Soon, it became too much, and I gradually walked down the mountain. I had this feeling that my mission was now complete. I had experienced what I had come there for, though I hadn't known what it was until that moment. I felt so very relaxed knowing that it was no longer necessary for me to endure the sufferings which occur with climbing to higher and higher altitudes. It was done. It was finished. I now looked forward to going back down with a renewed spirit. I felt love, Holy Spirit, and light surrounding me. My whole attitude had changed.

When I returned to the campsite, Pema could see that I was beaming. Our eyes met as if he knew. Without comment, he fixed me a delicious meal with some more tunafish slaw, good spicy soup, French fries, and tea. I ate heartily and asked for more. I was so happy, and for the first time, I could really say that I was truly enjoying the trip.

I spent the night in the little teahouse. It was not nearly so cold as sleeping on the icy ground even though it dropped way below freezing inside the room.

A lot of the people there were sick and going through the same dilemma as to whether or not they should stay there or go back down. I tried to help a young German boy who was very nauseated and afraid. I wished that I could have told others of my experience, but it was too personal.

How could I ever relate it to someone else?

Glaciers near Mount Everest

Mountains surrounding Everest.

DAY 10

I got up early and walked down to Pema's tent. He was already up and had breakfast almost ready — porridge, scrambled eggs, and bread warmed over the hot coals in the fireplace giving it a smoky flavor. After breakfast, we broke camp and started our descent on the icy trail. He arranged for the yak to come with someone else later after the sun began to thaw out some of the ice.

It seemed to be a thousand times easier going down to lower elevations. As usual, I wanted to hike alone. Pema obliged. I found myself reflecting on my mountaintop experience. Somehow I just felt good all over. Descending, we covered in one day what it took us three days to hike on ascending.

About midday, Pema was waiting on the trail ahead of me to discuss arrangements for lunch. He told me about a nunnery at Deboche where 16 Buddhist women lived. We went there. It was an old, two-story stone structure. Three ancient nuns were sitting in their smoky room while one peeled potatoes. They served us some good hot yak milk tea. I noticed they gave Pema a tin cup but gave me their only china cup.

We watched them going about their duties in the small kitchen where we sat. After the potatoes were peeled, they were boiled over the fire and then mashed up with a little flour, lots of garlic, and yak milk. They served it in a metal plate and put some kind of broth over it. I wanted so badly to take some pictures, but I knew they would forbid it. Older people thought that it would shorten their lives if anyone took their photographs.

After lunch, we walked together from the nunnery back to the Tengboche monastery. We arrived much earlier than we expected so we decided to keep on walking and spend the night beside the river at Pungo Tenga. It only took us seven hours to walk from Dengboche and seemed like a piece of cake all the way.

I went into the teahouse where I had stayed on my way up the trail and put my sleeping bag on the only cot left in the room. An American couple was resting there. We started talking. After a while, we finally got around to introducing ourselves to each other. She told me that she was Kathy Olsen and worked as a nurse at Pheriche.

I jumped out of my sleeping bag, grabbed her, and gave her a big hug. She was startled until I told her that the hug was a special request from President Carter.

Kathy was elated and flattered that he remembered her. She told me some of the stories of the Carter party. It was her opinion that all the Secret Servicemen had to be flown out by helicopter, not because they were sick from the altitude but were exhausted from having to guard the President all night long and then hike during the day. We laughed about the idea that the President needed to be guarded in that remote spot in the world, but we figured they could take no chances at all.

She had been in Nepal for two months, and her companion, a doctor named Dave Brook from Montana, was a volunteer who had been there for one month. They were both amazed that the former President was able to climb all the way to Kala Pattar.

Of course, the Presidential party had constant radio communication with Katmandu. If anyone got sick, they could call for a helicopter. This was certainly not available to anyone else. The Pheriche Clinic had no radio communication at all. If an ordinary trekker became deathly ill, they had to send their 48-year-old runner on a two-day hike all the way to Namche to report it to the police. The police would then radio the message to Katmandu. The embassy of the sick trekker would then be contacted to see if they would guarantee payment of a helicopter. If the embassy refused, then they didn't send it out. An insurance policy to pay for a helicopter evacuation could be purchased, but most often, people did not.

Apparently, the Nepalese government refused to place a radio at the Pheriche Clinic because it was so close to Tibet, and they did not want any communications between the Nepalese and the Tibetans. Kathy and Dave had pleaded with the President to try to persuade the King of Nepal to reconsider and put a radio there. It would save so many lives if they did not have to wait that long length of time for a runner to go all the way to Namche.

After the evening meal, I was getting into my sleeping bag when suddenly the door opened and there stood George. George was terribly fatigued and distressed. He and Malilapemba had made it to Lobuche, but George could not physically move another step. As far as he was concerned, the entire trip was ruined. His lifelong ambition of going to Kala Pattar was down the drain. Nothing that he had seen was worthy. The whole trip was a failure. I found it hard to listen to this nonsense, but did my best to console him.

DAY 11

I got up early, bid my American friends goodbye, and told George, Mailapemba, and Pema I would meet them down the trail. It was such a pretty day, and I enjoyed walking it alone. I stopped everyone on the trail I met. If they could speak a little English at all, then we had a discussion. If was fun to take it really easy and just do a lot of sitting, thinking, reading, and picture taking. The rest of them caught up with me just prior to the fork which leads up to Khumjung. George, Pema, and I decided to hike up to the Everest Hotel while Mailapemba took the short-cut back to Namche. From the trail, it was straight up all the way to the hotel.

The imposing structure sat on a hill at an altitude of about 14,000 feet. The Japanese built it in 1973, and it was a very plush stone structure. Every room in the hotel had a view of Mount Everest. Originally, their idea was to bring the rich Japanese tourists and helicopter them from Katmandu up to the hotel. The only problem, which they obviously did not consider, was that most all of the guests became sick and some even died. Though oxygen was provided in every room, one cannot fly into that high altitude and survive. It must be taken gradually.

Ironically, the only people who were able to use the hotel and enjoy it were the trekkers who acclimatized as they hiked up the mountains. It was closed in 1981 and had deteriorated badly. A Sherpa man was a caretaker in the hotel and served a light lunch with tea. The three of us had asparagus soup, fried rice, and tea. He told us that a new Japanese company had bought the hotel, and they were going to try to reopen it between October and May each year.

From May to October, the mountains are concealed by the monsoons. It made no sense to me to try this again unless they planned to assign a doctor to each hotel guest.

After lunch we walked down the mountain to Khumjung to see the school which Sir Edmund Hillery established. I talked with a couple of boys who were studying their math, and both of them could speak a few words of English. In addition to their native Sherpa language, they studied Nepalese, English, and Tibetan in school. I wondered how this learning might somehow affect their way of life. The people we had met were so innocent and naive in not knowing anything about the rest of the world; nor were they burdened with any of the world's problems.

George was still depressed and didn't want to go any further. He decided to turn back to Namche. Pema and I wanted to walk over to the Kunde Clinic. It was the only medical facility in the Khumbu region. This clinic was also built by Sir Edmund Hillery, who had become the New Zealand Ambassador to India and Nepal. I was told that Hillery occasionally visited the region but never proceeded any higher than the Kunde Clinic because he always got altitude sickness. The clinic was funded by the Canadian government, and they assigned a couple of doctors who served one-year stints to assist the Sherpas with medical problems. It must be similar to our Peace Corps. They were paid nothing other than just their expenses. Actually, this couple were both born in the United States but had later become Canadian citizens.

The woman doctor emphasized that they were there for the Sherpas — not the trekkers. Sherpas pay one rupee for a visit which is the equivalent of about five cents, somewhat different from an office visit to an American doctor. The hospital had no electricity, only a small generator in the back of the clinic. They had an old X-ray machine, but didn't use it unless it was absolutely necessary. It was too costly to run the generator. They could give a blood test, but it had to be done on a hand-cranked centrifuge taking about 20 minutes to spin it out.

They mostly had to treat their patients for tuberculosis, then pneumonia, and, beyond that, a lot of fractures and cuts.

Occasionally, they delivered babies, but it was against Sherpa customs for a woman to let anyone else know that she was pregnant. It was considered to be bad luck. They wore such loose clothing that a pregnancy would probably not be noticed. If a woman was having trouble delivering the baby, she would send for the doctor who had to slip into the house at night or when no one else could see. The pregnant women simply refused to come to the hospital; they were afraid that someone might see their bodies.

The doctors also tried to educate people in the area on birth control. The population was exploding in Nepal. Most of them knew nothing of birth control. The World Health Organization permitted them to use an injection on the women, not permitted in the United States. This injection every three months prevented pregnancy.

The doctors said that it was difficult to get the women to come to the clinic to receive the injection. They had tried using an I.U.D., but Sherpa women would not permit the doctor to give them a vaginal examination.

The doctor also told me that Sherpas usually

don't marry until they are in their mid-20's. This is
because they do not reach puberty until they are
around 18 years old. In the past, most marriages
were always arranged. But this custom was beginning to go by the wayside. The boy's parents are
required to make a gift of a dowry to the girl's parents, which is the opposite of the Hindu tradition in
India. Once a Sherpa couple is married, they may
separate or divorce only if no children have been
born and the husband gives some possessions to his
wife. However, once a baby has been born, it is
impossible to ever separate or divorce.

The doctor said that Sherpas are considered by
all of the other Nepalese to be the wealthiest people
in the country since there are so many trekkers who
have come into the area in the past ten years. A
porter can make 50 to 60 rupees a day (approximately $3.00), which was very good money. Lhakpa
told me that he only made 35 rupees a day, about
$2.00.

The doctors do not see any malaria at this high
altitude. But it is very prevalent in southern Nepal,
as well as meningitis and hepatitis. The only other
real medical problem they have to deal with in the
Khumbu region is diarrhea and dysentery because
of the *giardia* (amoebic parasite) in the water.

After leaving the Kunde hospital, Pema and I
walked down to Syangboche, the location of an air
strip. We stopped at a small teahouse where a
woman, who had eight small children, served us a
cup of hot yak milk tea. She had obviously not been
visiting the hospital at Kunde for her injections.

I asked Pema to go on ahead; I wanted to take a
leisurely walk down the mountain to Namche. The
sun was setting, and it was such a beautiful sight to

behold. I felt the need to soak up as much of the surroundings as possible because the time was getting short.

Occasionally stopping and sitting on a rock, I watched the last bit of sun drop behind the mountains. I wanted to capture that memory and hold it in my treasure chest of beautiful sights in this world. It was well after dark when I arrived at the Namche teahouse.

Lhakpa and Mary were there. They had been in Namche ever since Mary had gotten sick. She said that the descent had not helped her and she had continued to be nauseous, with headaches and diarrhea. George was sick physically, mentally, and emotionally. I didn't want to be around them because it made me feel guilty that I felt so good.

Mailapemba could see it in my eyes that I was a different person from the one he left in Dengboche. As a result, he decided to reward me with a glass of chang. I tasted it and knew there was no way I could drink it. It is made from soured rice and is thick and milky-looking. I didn't want to offend him, but I had to pass it up.

DAY 12

Snow was falling. The decision had been made by all of us to head back to Lukla. I had mixed emotions about leaving Namche. I felt fine and there were so many things in the area to see. I walked on ahead of the others and met a German boy going down the trail as well. He told me of his hike to Gokyo and the beautiful lake there. From one side of the lake, Mount Everest could be seen, and he said it was a most splendid sight. He spoke of the beauty of watching the sunset as well as the sunrise over the lake with the snowcapped mountains in the background.

What surprised me was that he had no camera. He felt a camera couldn't do justice to such beauty, and he wanted to keep the photographs only in his mind. I felt somewhat envious. It was only a day or two hike to Gokyo, and I wanted to see that beautiful spot, too. You can't see it all, I decided; maybe on the next trip, I could do that.

It was certainly easier walking down to the river compared to what it was like coming up from the river. But the detour with little narrow trails running up and down the embankments above the river were worse than I had remembered. Someone told us of an American man who fell the day before, breaking his neck and back. His wife was with him, and they had to get volunteers to retrieve him and bodily carry him back to Lukla. There was no telling how much damage they did to him in carrying him, but his wife couldn't leave him on the side of the mountain.

George caught up with me; he, Pema, and I walked together for a distance. George was complaining every foot of the way. He had eaten no meat since he left Katmandu, and he wanted a chicken. At every house we passed, he made Pema bargain with the woman of the house to try to buy one chicken, but no one wanted to sell.

The chickens were used by these people for laying eggs and not for eating. Finally, after some woman refused to sell her chicken, George told Pema to offer her 100 rupees ($6.00). With that, the woman quickly ran into the yard and caught the little scrawny chicken before the fool changed his mind.

We walked to Phakding (8,700 feet), to the little

house next to the Dudh Kosi River, where we had stayed the first night. The area adjacent to the house set aside for camping was the spot where we had camped. It seemed so funny that the temperature was about the same that day as it was the day we arrived when I almost froze to death. Compared to what we had been accustomed to, it felt like a summer day. The body is indeed a most versatile object and generally adapts well.

Pema prepared a great chicken curry for George, which he and Mary devoured. Pema, always thoughtful, made me a nice vegetable curry, without the chicken. It really tasted good over rice. Pema had found what he called a tangerine that was as green as a lime. Mary said it was a mandarin. It still looked and tasted like a tangerine, except for the color. This was used to make the curry taste more tangy.

DAY 13

I slept very well compared to the first night when we camped there. I had no nightmarish dreams.

Early the next morning, I was awakened by George who shouted from his sleeping bag next to me, "Damn, I thought I'd lost it."

I pretended to be asleep and didn't respond, but I knew what had happened. In very high altitudes men are impotent. I was told that in the spring the couples who lived way up in the mountain villages would have to come down to the valley for breeding purposes. We had obviously reached a low enough altitude for George to recover from this malady.

It was only a three-hour walk from Phakding by the river back up the mountain to Lukla. This was our last hiking day, and I had some regrets knowing

that this once-in-a-lifetime experience was coming
to an end.

Mary and I took the final walk together. George,
in his usual haste, and the Sherpas, who were anxious to return to their families, rushed up the mountain trail. Time was no object for us, so we enjoyed
spending a leisurely period walking and talking.

Mary was a deeply religious person, steeped in
the dogma of the Episcopal Church. She was a lay
reader and a real worker in her church community.
What I found incongruous was the way she constantly worried. We had a discussion about that,
and I told her my philosophy. If a person really has
faith in God, then it is sacrilegious to worry. It is like
saying, "I'm not sure if God is going to take care of
this situation." "Don't be anxious for tomorrow, let
tomorrow be anxious for itself."

I feel that it is my responsibility to do the very
best that I can in every given situation, and then it is
imperative that I surrender all of the rest, including
the results, to God. As long as I have done my best,
then there is really nothing else to worry about. God
always seems to provide and take care of me. This
was the tenor of our conversation and made for a
most pleasant walk as we enjoyed the beauty of the
flora and fauna along the trail.

When we arrived at Lukla, it seemed that my
philosophy was going to be tested. Over 300 people
were waiting to get out of there. No plane had been in
for over three days because of the bad weather. The
fog seemed to get thicker and thicker that afternoon.

We pitched our tents, and I decided to indulge
myself in a long-overdue shower. My hair was so
greasy that when I took my wool hat off, George
wanted to take a picture of it. I admit it did look

funny, but where we had been I was not very concerned with my looks.

This small teahouse had a sign in front which read, "Hot Showers." I went in, and they said it would take about 30 minutes to an hour to heat the water. It was heated in a large kettle over the fire. While waiting, I sat and drank tea with a group of Germans who were speaking of their hiking experiences.

The shower felt wonderful. I pulled the chain and let the warm water wet my body. I then turned it off to soap up, and hoped that there would be enough water left to get the soap off. This was accomplished in a little stall in the unheated basement where the temperature hovered around freezing. I didn't care, I felt cleaner, and my hair had some of the oil out of it.

I went back to the tent where I found Mary and George talking to a Swedish couple they had met in Namche. We decided to play cards together inside the tent. A candle was used for light and heat. Later hot tea was served by our wonderful Sherpa hosts.

While playing cards, we heard the sound of a helicopter coming through the fog. All of the waiting throngs of people ran out of their tents and rushed to the adjacent airstrip. A group of American men jumped on the helicopter. They apparently had chartered it for $2,000. Only 11 passengers could go. We agreed that a helicopter may be better than waiting for about a week which a lot of those people had done. Some got tired of waiting and had left for Jiri, a six-day walk from Lukla and a 13-hour bus ride from Katmandu.

DAY 14

The fog and clouds still lingered. Another helicopter came but no planes. I talked to the pilot. He said he needed $2,000, and no more than 11 passengers. There were already two helicopters booked ahead. With this weather, nobody had any idea when we might leave. I decided to get a pad and go around gathering names of people who wanted to cough up that much money to get back to Katmandu. I quickly signed up 11 people. Then I talked with Pasang, who is Lhakpa's older brother.

Pasang had some connection with the airlines. He was the brightest Sherpa I had met. He spoke very good English and had even been outside Nepal. After he had served as a guide on a Swiss and French hiking team, they paid his way to visit them in France and Switzerland. He had hiked up Annapurna with several expeditions and had been on an Everest expedition with Austrians. Anyway, Pasang had an "in" with the airlines, and I sought his help.

I decided to call a meeting of my 11 signers at the Panorama Lodge, the teahouse where I had taken my shower the day before. The 11 people consisted of Australians, Germans, French, and Canadians; I was the only American. Everyone seemed eager to pay the price since the weather looked rotten with no hope of clearing. We had all been talking to people who had been waiting there for five, six, and seven days.

If you had a confirmed flight for a particular day, and the weather was clear enough for the planes to come in, then you could board the plane regardless of how many days others may have been waiting there. If the day you were confirmed passed by without a plane coming in, then you were put at the bottom of the waiting list, and it could take five or six days, depending on the weather. The planes could only take 15 passengers, and even on a good day, there were only three scheduled flights.

Some of our group decided to order a bottle of spirits. No one had had any alcohol since they left Katmandu, and the consensus was that it would be nice to jazz up the hot tea a little bit. After the spirits had warmed our stomachs and dulled our brains, we fell into a long conversation which resulted in an argument about future Sherpa life. The question was a good one.

Do you educate these Sherpa people, bring in electricity, television, radio, telephones, and all of the world's modern equipment and "bring them up to date?" They had been living without this technology for thousands of years. According to all statistics, they live in abject poverty. Since none of them made more than $100 a year, certainly they qualified in everyone's statistic book as being "poor." The only problem is, they were not aware of it. They didn't seem to want anything more and appeared to be happy.

I can see the argument for having better medical services so that they can have a longer life span and lower their infant mortality. But it would be such a shame to spoil the innocence of their smiles by watching the nightly news on TV with all of the world's problems. I guess eventually it will come. I feel very fortunate that I was able to see these people and know them in all of their naivete. There was even talk of building a road from Jiri to Lukla and possibly on up the valley toward Everest. That would be a crime in my book. How could we possibly allow this tranquillity to be destroyed by the sounds of trucks, buses, cars, and pollution? However, we have done it to the rest of the world, so I am sure that the Khumbu region will be next.

DAY 15

I was lying in my sleeping bag at 5:00 a.m. wondering what the day would bring. This was the day that I was confirmed with a plane reservation to fly back to Katmandu. Is it possible that my Dennard luck would hold up and allow me to leave as scheduled, or would I wait for the chartered helicopters that were making a killing on all of the tourists?

The helicopters were army or government helicopters, not privately owned. And I wondered about where that $2,000 was going. My wondering got the best of me. I threw open the tent flap. To my utter amazement, there it was in all of it's glory — the sun rising! The skies were perfectly clear. What had I done to deserve all of this?

I began to get excited about leaving and realized that this breakfast with George and Mary would probably be our last meal together. I had a talk with Lhakpa and Mailapemba. I let them know how good they had been to me and how much I appreciated all of their care and assistance. I gave a very special hug to Pema and asked him if there was anything that I could do for him. He said that if I ever came back to please bring some clothes for his children. You cannot mail anything to Lukla or send any parcels in the mail to Nepal. A large amount of duty would have to be paid in order to receive it. That was money they didn't have. I promised Pema that if I ever heard of anyone going to Lukla, I would certainly send him something.

We all took pictures and, during the photography session, I heard people cheering and clapping their hands. You could hear the sounds of the airplanes coming in, the first in six days. Everyone was running around elated. I felt guilty that I was on the first plane leaving with all of those 300 plus people who had been waiting there for a week trying to get out.

I jumped on the plane, trying to contain my excitement. The pilot never cut off the motor and only stopped for about two minutes. Everyone else boarded as fast as possible, and the plane spun around and took off down the hill. There was a 2,000-foot drop-off at the end of the runway, so we kept our fingers crossed hoping the plane would get airborne. I looked back over my shoulder through the window and caught a glimpse of the waving hands from those left behind. I visualized those Sherpa smiles with a desire to permanently imprint them in my mind. A sensation of fulfillment overwhelmed me knowing that I had just completed my lifetime dream.

TED,
THE BEEKEEPER

C H A P T E R 3

TED, THE BEEKEEPER

I was sitting on Winston's bench trying to figure out whether it was Wednesday or Thursday. That is one of the greatest benefits of being on vacation. Time has no meaning. Watches can be discarded.

The crystal blue sea is the primary view from the little grass hut where we had spent the night, but the lushness of green was constantly in my periphery. Bunches of bananas hung from stalks in every direction and almond trees provided shade from the hot sun. Coconuts, papayas, mangos, pineapple, breadfruit, and soursop abound making this a paradise for fruit lovers. I kept having to pinch myself to see if I had died and gone to heaven.

My son, Ted, had been in Jamaica for 15 months serving a 27-month tour of duty in the Peace Corps. This worthwhile organization started by President Kennedy attracts volunteers of all ages to help where needed in developing countries. Ted teaches the art of beekeeping to school children, church groups, and others who want to learn. Honey is a product that will bring needed income into this poor country where there is 90 percent unemployment.

Ted's territory is St. Mary Parish, which incorporates a portion of the Blue Mountain chain and stretches to the Caribbean Sea on the north coast. Highgate is a little mountain village that he now calls home. His blond hair and light skin make him an oddball among the black population. But he has now been accepted by them. They yell, "Hey, Ted!" as he rides his motor scooter up the pot-holed streets, a far cry from the more derogatory catcalls he heard when he first arrived. The natives don't seem to understand why a young man just out of college would give up that much of his life trying to help other people. They question his motives and have even accused him of being with the dreaded American CIA.

We drove a rental car to the north coast to visit Winston, one of Ted's beekeepers. He is a thin, fortyish-looking man with coal-black skin and long dread locks. He lives alone in a little grass hut about 500 feet up the mountain. His view of the ocean would be worth hundreds of thousands of dollars in America. But he is one of many impoverished squatters who live on the mostly undeveloped northern coastline.

We accepted Winston's invitation to stay overnight, a real experience for me that would not be available, and probably not desirable, to most tourists. It's not possible to drive to his hut. We had to walk a couple of miles along a path where the road ran out. No electricity or modern conveniences mar the naturalness of this setting.

A fire was built with sticks to cook the tasty evening meal, which consisted of stir-fried vegetables from his garden and spiced with scotch-bonnet peppers, the hottest ever produced. He blessed the food and praised Jah (God) for providing it. I know very little about his Rastafarian religion,

Beekeepers

but I did recognize the word "Selah" at the end of his prayer. We echoed it back to him.

The food was delicious. We cooled our palates with a mint tea sweetened with his honey and drank from a coconut shell. There was much conversation, most of which Ted had to interpret for me. Their patois language is a mixture of English and African dialects. Fortunately, Ted not only understands it, but can speak it right back to them. This makes the white boy, as they call him, much more acceptable.

With full bellies, we moved outside the hut under a sky filled with millions of stars. Winston built a fire and we sat around it as if it were cold. Actually, their temperature rarely goes below 60 or above 80, so the fire was mostly for atmosphere.

Winston went inside the hut and dragged out a large flour sack about the size of one of our 30-gallon garbage bags. It contained his stash of marijuana that grows higher up in the mountains. He rolled a joint the size of a large cigar and passed it to us like the Indian peace pipe. We explained to him that we are nonsmokers, although we didn't want to offend him. He understood, and we swapped stories until sleep overtook me. The mattress, consisting of a pile of palm fronds, seemed as comfortable as a bed.

Sunrise found us taking a refreshing dip in the ocean. We swam out to a rock and sat there talking about the unabashed beauty of this place and the simplicity of Winston's lifestyle that appears to be so innocent and far removed from the problems of the world. There is no TV, radio, or newspaper to upset his spirit and convince him that people are evil. His world is bright and was only interrupted by a passer-by riding on a donkey and leading a few goats on a rope. They chatted about God knows what, because there is no understanding their talk with each other. The old man rode off leaving Winston time to prepare our breakfast. A leafy vegetable similar to turnip greens and boiled bananas is typically what Jamai-cans eat in the morning. I found this to be a satisfy-ing departure from my usual bowl of cereal.

After our swim, I walked up the beach and found a grassy spot under an almond tree where cows grazed. I wallowed around in the cool grass the way my dog and I do at home, followed by a short nap. Win-ston called me to come up for a tall glass of soursop, a spiny fruit with a tart edible pulp. Still being thirsty, he found me an unripe coconut filled with about a quart of clear liquid that occurs before the meat forms. This would quench anyone's thirst cravings.

It came time to bid Winston farewell. On parting, a man balls his fist and touches it against the fist of the other saying, "Re'spect," with a heavy accent on

Coffee beans

the first syllable. It was with great sincerity that I made the gesture; I did respect him. He was a good man.

Our next stop was a visit to "THE COFFEE MAN." His house is high up in the Blue Mountains between 4,000-5,000 feet elevation with a spectacular view of the valley below. The abundant coffee trees are tended by him each day. When the coffee bean has reached its desired reddish color, it is picked by hand and placed in the shucker to remove the skin. It is roasted to the exact moment of perfection and then cured.

We were invited in for a cup of the best coffee in the world. It had been aged for 12 years, making it much more mellow. The Jamaican coffee co-op requires all growers to sell only to them. All the coffees are mixed together and sold, mostly to the Japanese. It's expensive stuff. My daughter saw a package of Blue Mountain coffee in an Atlanta delicatessen for $40.00 a pound.

Horace, the Coffee Man, refuses to sell to the co-op because his product is far superior and he feels that it should be kept separate. So, he is left to sell illegally only to friends who know about him. The aroma of the brewing pot would make even nondrinkers drool. Neither Ted nor I drink coffee, but both of us had a second cup. Ted had warned me not to insult him by using sugar or cream. Horace is a purist from the word go. He served us biscuits and honey from his hives. Because the bees had feasted on the blooms of the coffee trees, the honey had a taste of coffee that made it unusual but good.

Horace liked Ted because he said the Peace Corps is doing a very fine thing for his country. They talked bee talk for a while. I was anxious to buy some of his product to take home, but I offended him when I pulled out my wallet.

He filled my arms with six bags of the valuable beans and said, "Thank you for letting your son be in the Peace Corps."

I swelled with pride as we started out on that long curvy road going back down the mountain.

Beautiful bougainvillea of many colors and coral vine grew wild like weeds next to the road. The flame of the forest trees are also abundant. It is a real sight for flower lovers. As we drove along, a multitude of people stood beside the road hitchhiking. It is considered rude to pass them by if you have room, which to them means about ten people crammed in a car. We picked up three older women dressed to the nines in their white dresses and hats on the way to church. It was Saturday afternoon, and Ted told me that the Seventh Day Adventist Church is really big there. Their sabbath is on Saturday.

My eyes were constantly perusing the spectacular scenery. We passed large groves of bamboo, some of it as much as six inches in diameter. I made the statement that I had always wanted big bamboo. I thought it was very attractive and there were so many uses for it. Our passengers in the back seat were cracking up, and Ted was snickering. He quickly changed the subject. Later he told me that bamboo was the Jamaican word for a man's private part and that I had thoroughly embarrassed him in front of the ladies. I kept my mouth shut from then on.

We drove by numerous rum bars where men gather to swig that potent drink that is produced from their numerous sugar cane fields. There were just as many jerk chicken stands along the road where meat is smoked with a blistering hot barbecue sauce. Driving along with the windows down and listening to reggae music on the radio still lingers in my mind. All of these sounds, smells, and sights give a stranger like me the flavor of a country.

We were tired when we got back to Ted's place, but we had to carry buckets of water from the backyard cistern to have a bath.

As I started to undress, I glanced down at my body and yelled, "What are these black things on me?"

There were no less than 300 seed ticks that had attached themselves from my head to my toes. We spent over two hours with tweezers pulling out what the Jamaicans call "grass lice." They are the size of ground black pepper. My morning snooze in the grass was the likely sight of the crime. Ted said that you find these varmints wherever cows have been.

He had never seen any person or animal that had as many as I did. Surely pain is better than your whole body itching at one time. I was in misery.

The next morning Ted tried to convince me to ride on the back of his motor scooter, but I wanted no part of it. The ticks had caused me to have nausea and diarrhea. At his unyielding insistence, I reluctantly crawled on the trail bike, donned a helmet, and we took off for parts unknown. The narrow road full of pot holes went straight down the mountain where a stream brought it to an end. As we walked along the jungly path, I was informed that we were going to visit the root doctor. Had I been well, this would have been a wonderful hike, but my mood made me long for a bed.

Finally, we arrived and were met by a woman named Clara with a mound of dread locks, bright loving eyes, and a toothy grin. She hugged me because I was Ted's father. He helps her tend a number of bee hives. My stomach felt sick and I excused myself to head for the nearest bushes. It was a false alarm, so I returned to her grass hut. She met me holding a cup of "tea" in her outstretched hand.

I shook my head. "I can't put anything in my mouth because if I do it's going to come right back up."

She smiled and said, "Drink it."

I looked at Ted, and he nodded his head, insisting that I obey her command. I lifted the cup to my mouth, and it had a bitter taste. There's no way for me to swallow this stuff, I thought. They both stared at me, reminiscent of my mother standing over me with the medicine bottle when I was a child. I bravely turned it up and guzzled down the last drop of the unpalatable potion. To my absolute and utter amazement, within ten seconds the nausea was

Ted and Clara

gone. No signs of it remained. It had vanished in thin air and never returned.

She mixed up a salve that appeared to have charcoal in it and smelled of menthol and camphor. When it was rubbed on the multitude of bites, the itching ceased immediately. I was now a convert and wanted to spend some time talking with her, but Ted had to move on to his next client.

As an old American custom, I reached for my wallet, but she laughed. Instead, she placed a gift in my hand that looked like a bag of dried oak leaves to make the tea to use as a tonic. She warned me that my insides would be shaking in a day or two. She was right again. They did. But the tea worked wonders. After kissing me on the cheek, she whispered that healing is the work of God. I felt so thankful for what had been done for me.

A few days later as my plane took off heading

north, I looked back to see that small island down in the Caribbean where Winston, Horace, Clara, and others like them live. I could visualize Ted on his motor scooter, making house calls all around St. Mary Parish, and felt comforted to know that my son was having experiences that will be with him for a lifetime. We call these people poor because materially they have nothing in comparison to us. But they are rich in spirit and have a simple way of life that we mistakenly abandoned.

JEFF AND I

Photo: My son, Jeff, and I

CHAPTER 4

JEFF AND I

In February, when I visited Jeff in Boston (where he attended Boston University), we planned a hiking trip out West. He complained about his need to get out of the city and see some nature. It was his suggestion that we make it a twosome, a sort of father-son thing. That is the ultimate flattery for any father to have his 21-year-old son act as if he wants to be with only him. We talked about going to Yosemite in California between his spring semester and summer school, but my old body had other ideas.

I managed to injure my right knee on a canoe trip down the Satilla River during Ted's spring break. I kept thinking it would get better, but it never did, so the middle of April found me on the operating table for orthoscopic surgery. Recovery was not sufficient by late May, so we rescheduled our trip for mid-August after his summer school session.

My sister and her husband, who is a physics professor at the University of Houston, visit Los Alamos, New Mexico, each year in the summer for him to work in the lab. This seemed like a good time to combine a long-overdue visit with them and the hike with Jeff. So Marie and I went out early and spent five enjoyable days with them seeing Northern New Mexico. It was, as they say, truly the Land of Enchantment.

We visited Jemez Springs where we viewed ruins of sixteenth-century Spanish churches, Bandelier National Monument with its ancient Indian cliff dwellings, Taos and the nearby Indian Pueblo, toured the capital city of Santa Fe, and ate marvelous native New Mexican cuisine with its red and green chili peppers. This gave us a sufficient taste of New Mexico to let us know that we wanted to someday return.

Marie flew back home and Jeff arrived in Albuquerque. We immediately motored up to Santa Fe. He had never been to an opera so that evening we attended the famous Opera House for a stunning performance of *La Traviata*. The theater is situated on a hill north of town and is a unique architectural spectacle. Those who do not want to pay the $50 to $100 for a seat purchase standing room tickets for $5. After the first act, all the people who had been standing, rush for the vacant seats.

Santa Fe is a rather trendy place where yuppies and jet-setters gather in the summer for the great ballets, theater, symphony, and such. It has maintained the old Spanish and Indian flavor by having very strict zoning. All buildings seem to be no more than two stories high and are clay-colored in the adobe style.

We slept at the hostel where we were given complimentary overnights because I knew the owner. He had stayed in my hostel about a year previously.

The purpose of the trip was to hike in the mountains, not sight-seeing in the city. So we headed up to Pilar, located on the Rio Grande just ten miles south of Taos, the famous ski resort. Dick Thibodeaux, an acquaintance of mine, and his partner, Robin Sanders, operated a bed and breakfast with separate facilities for a hostel. They invited us for dinner to eat some very delicious stir-fried vegetables.

After dinner we walked up to the top of the mesa about 1,000 feet straight up to view a lunar eclipse. Several other guests joined us for the hike to see this infrequent spectacle. It was a beautiful evening with enough chill in the air to wear a sweater. The eclipse was interesting, but we mainly enjoyed just being with the people.

Dick had worked with Sierra Club expeditions and was familiar with good hiking trails in the area. He pointed out some places on the map that he thought we'd enjoy hiking. He and Robin were extremely helpful in advising us where to go and what supplies to take.

The next morning they drove us into the mountains to begin our long-awaited father-son hike. The surrounding mountains were thick with trees such as spruce and aspen, although further south the mountains were treeless. Being an extension of the Rockies, they are locally referred to as the Sangre de Cristo (Blood of Christ) Mountains. We had purchased a map from the forest rangers in Santa Fe detailing the Pecos Wilderness area, a part of the Carson and Santa Fe National Forests.

We drove up an old logging road #161 in our fancy Dodge Spirit rental car. The trail begins where the road ends at 9600 feet elevation. I was having some reminiscent thoughts about my experiences in the Himalayas with altitude sickness.

Dick and Robin hiked with us for about an hour.

The trail was switchbacking as we gained altitude. Wildflowers, brightly colored yellow, red, and blue, were abundant, but I couldn't identify the names of any of them.

After they turned back, Jeff and I, being all alone, looked for a nice log to have our first meal. We had shopped at the Food Emporium in Santa Fe and purchased a variety of dried foods such as spaghetti, lentils, rice, dried fruits, a couple of cans of fish, and some packaged seasonings to make the food palatable.

We opened a can of herring, soaked in tomato sauce, which didn't taste too bad with some cheese and bread. As we finished, it began to rain, so we pulled out our ponchos. It then began to turn bitter cold, something I am unaccustomed to in August. We could really feel it, since we had started the hike in shorts and T-shirts.

We put on more clothes and draped garbage bags over our backpacks to continue upward on the trail. The rain began to turn into ice and before long we were being peppered with hail. The temperature must have dropped to around the freezing point; the hail stones didn't melt. They covered the trail and we were walking in a sea of white. The ice pebbles were banking up on the trees and also on my Australian outback hat. The harsh weather was unrelenting for over an hour, but we kept trudging upward knowing that it was too cold to stop.

We were about to get discouraged until we arrived at a sign directing us to Serpent Lake, at 12,000 feet. We descended to "the lake," actually about the size of the pond at the Hostel.

This was our planned destination for the first night. Grass about six inches in height grew around the lake, and it appeared to be soft ground for the

tent. However, large stones were embedded in the
soil, and we really had to search for a good soft place
to pitch the tent.

We were happy to have found a spot that had
beautiful scenery, or "a room with a view." While we
were making a clearing on the ice-sprinkled grass to
erect the tent, we were suddenly startled by a large
black animal coming toward us about 50 feet away.
Fortunately, it turned out to be a friendly cow. She
walked right up to us with her big inquisitive eyes to
check us out.

We had a good laugh because we were very
much aware that this was bear country. Soon our
new friend was joined by about ten of her compatri-
ots. They all joined us and watched as we set up the
tent. Jeff, knowing that I am a "country boy" from
Pineview, thought I should milk one of the cows to
have fresh milk for supper. But I wasn't the least bit
interested.

It was still sprinkling rain and ice, so we put on
dry clothes and climbed into our sleeping bags to
warm up.

Dinner consisted of lentils cooked on our little
backpacking stove at the front door of the tent. We
didn't even get out of our sleeping bags. The temperature really began to drop when the sun went
down behind the mountains.

I thought of the contrast in weather at home in
August which was probably 95 degrees and 99-
percent humidity. Here it was so cold.

Before sunset it cleared off, giving us a brilliant
view of the surrounding mountains. The lake sits in
the bottom of a bowl rimmed with 13,000-foot me-
sas. Mesa means "table" in Spanish, and it is easy to
understand how they get the name. When you see

the tops of them, they are as flat as a landing strip.

The full moon began to rise, and we prepared to settle in for a long sleep. Unfortunately, that did not happen. The rain returned and stayed with us all night long. I have camped so many times in pouring rain that I never go off without a piece of plastic to put underneath the tent and one to cover the top of it. This has kept me dry more times than I can remember, and fortunately it did again.

We were told that in New Mexico the average annual rainfall was about 10-12 inches. It seems that we received about half of that in one night.

Morning came but the rain continued. The fog had moved down into the bowl, so there was no longer any view of the mountains. We had planned to hike up to Jicarita Peak at 12,834 feet. Serpent Lake is at 11,640 feet, so it would not be too strenuous.

Our hiking boots were soaked as well as our packs. It seemed best to wait it out. Locals had warned us that the only adverse weather to expect would be those afternoon thunderstorms with some intense lightning. What we were experiencing seemed more like a winter's rain that had set in for days. The temperature was probably in the 30's, certainly no more than 40 degrees.

Ted, my son with the religion major, had given me a book to read on the trip with the admonition that, in his opinion, I definitely needed to read it. It is called *Zen Mind, Beginners Mind*, by Shunryu Suzuki.

Jeff and I took turns reading aloud followed by an intense discussion. The essence of it is the need to find perfection out of imperfection and to find truth through difficulties and suffering. Pleasure should not be different from difficulty. Good should not be different from bad. We should find pleasure in suffering. Both of us agreed that an opportunity had been given us to put this philosophy into practice. Being in a small, two-person backpacking tent is pretty close quarters. There is no room to move around. We just enjoyed the warmth of our sleeping bags and read and slept and munched on dried fruit and gorp.

Jeff was reading *The Education Of Little Tree* by Forrest Carter. It is a story of a Cherokee Indian boy, orphaned as a small child, who was sent to live with his grandparents in the North Carolina mountains. They taught him the ways of the Cherokee and how to respect nature and the Earth. Even though I had already read it, we switched off reading it aloud together.

This book brought back so many memories for me growing up in Pineview. Like him, I had spent much time with my grandparents who lived behind our house. They used to tell me about their childhoods. Both of them were born in the 1880s when the South was under reconstruction and times were hard.

I told Jeff about the night my grandfather fell down the back steps of the house and never regained consciousness before he died a few days later. I was the only one with him. It was such a traumatic experience for me as an eight-year-old because I loved him so much. Trying to tell this story brought out emotions in me that obviously had been suppressed for many years. I was unable to finish telling the story. We just lay there a long time without speaking. Finally, the rain stopped and we both agreed to move on. Maybe Serpent Lake had been cursed with evil spirits in some way, so that it only rained there and nowhere else.

For the first time on the trip, I pulled out the old

quartz clock from the pack to check the time. It was 12:40. The rain had been falling for about 24 hours and had now subsided. The ground was soaked. It was my turn to read to Jeff from my book:

> "Some people are annoyed when they are lying in their beds in the mornings because they do not know that later they will see the beautiful sun rising from the east. If our mind is concentrated on ourselves, we will have this kind of worry. But if we accept ourselves as the embodiment of the truth, we will have no worry. We will think that now it is raining but we do not know what will happen in the next moment. By the time we go out, it may be a beautiful day or a stormy day. Since we do not know, let's appreciate the sound of the rain now. This is the right kind of attitude. If you understand yourself as a temporal embodiment of the truth, you will have no difficulty whatsoever. You will appreciate your surroundings and yourself even in the midst of difficulties."

This convinced us to pack it all up in quick fashion and move out. As we hiked up the mountain, streaks of blue began appearing in the cloudy skies, and it seemed that clearing was imminent.

We reached a fork in the trail with no marking. I argued that the trail going downward was the one to take, but Jeff was convinced that we should take the upward trail. It seemed to me that his suggestion would lead us up to Jicarita Peak, and because of the weather, we had abandoned that idea. I didn't mind the climb up the peak, but since we would have to back track, I wanted to stash the packs. So we bet a beer on who was right. Jeff learned to read contour maps on his Outward Bound trip in the Colorado Rockies after his junior year of high school.

I yielded and we carried the packs and switch-backed upward to cross over the humpback mountain. When we reached the top, there was a marker which proved him right. I asked forbearance from having to pay off the bet for that night but agreed to buy him any kind of beer he wanted when we returned to what some people refer to as civilization.

The top of the mountain was extremely windy and cold. We had on jackets, hats, and gloves. Back to the east of us was clear sky, but a mean black cloud was moving in from the west. We wanted to get off that mountain as quickly as possible before the lightning started.

An alternative trail follows around the perimeter of the mountain in a horseshoe shape, which would give some fantastic views. It was much too windy and cold, and we needed to get off the top of that mountain before the lightning storm.

The descent from the summit was along a rocky trail to the tree line at about 12,000 feet. Before too long, the clouds had passed by and the views were spectacular. We took a few pictures and occasionally stopped along the way to view nature's outbursts of wildflowers. There were small streams that made it handy to replenish our water supply. We had three canteens and a plastic gallon milk jug that Dick had given us. Since Jeff forgot to bring the water filter, we were using iodine tablets to kill *giardia*. Luckily we brought along a package of powdered Gatorade to cut the taste of the iodine.

The trail continued downward through a sea of

aspens. Their pale greenish-yellow bark had been marred by thoughtless hikers who had carved their initials.

We lunched on tuna fish, bread, and cheese while basking in the sun. When Jeff and I are alone, we sometimes share intimate thoughts. He expressed concern about his love life, and I am not too old to remember those same gnawing concerns. These interludes are what make a trip like this so special. We both get a chance to delve into each other's psyche.

We discovered a great campsite down by a stream with small waterfalls. It reminded me of the spot in North Carolina where Marie and I go camping, except the altitude of this one was 10,600 feet. When it's cold enough to wear a down jacket, I can easily talk myself out of taking a bath in the stream. There is always *mañana*.

Jeff wanted a campfire. He gathered wood while I cooked up some brown rice mixed with dried soup mixture. The setting sun illumined the mountaintop that we had earlier crossed. The spectacular view was certainly worthy of a few photos.

Our surprise for the day was the sighting of three horses coming up the trail crossing over the stream; one of them was being ridden by what I would call a real western cowboy. This was our first viewing of a human being since we left Dick and Robin.

While the horses drank from the stream, we got acquainted. He operates a wilderness trip for those who are willing to pay $500 to take them off to a campsite somewhere up there in the Pecos Wilderness. I was amused that he requires his clients to walk and packs the horses with their gear.

The California couple he had just deposited at 12,000 feet were excited, he said. I couldn't help but

Jicarita Peak

wonder about lowlanders going up to such a high altitude for their first night of camping. He handed me his card which gave his name as Clay Gibbard. He allowed as how he had left Michigan in 1965 and came to this area where he bought 40 acres and a mule. He claimed that he always liked to rough it, but had to change his ways a little when he married a woman who insisted on a flushing toilet. "You know how these women are," he said.

His skin was reddish-brown like an Indian's and bushy hairs were growing out of his ears. He felt that we looked too pale and hoped we were not having some altitude problems.

We laughed as he rode off into the sunset trailing the other horses behind him. Old Clay Gibbard truly loved this place and we both could easily understand it.

The evening dinner consisted of seasoned rice with a little cheese and bread on the side. Jeff worked on getting the campfire started, but wet wood is difficult to get going. We both decided that the almost full moon rising over the mountain was far more beautiful than a campfire. The moonlight was so bright that it lighted up our camp area like a Coleman lantern. We could almost read by it. All of the heavenly bodies are so much brighter in the higher elevations. Jeff talked about his astronomy class he had just completed in summer school. We laid on our backs gazing at the stars while talking and sipping a little hot cranberry tea spiked with brandy, until we were mellow and warm.

How sweet it is to get out of a tent in the morning and see the sun in a cloudless sky. But we have learned that New Mexico weather is not to be trusted. It is as fickle as a smiling grizzly bear. The grass was being dried by the warm sun, and we sat there munching on oatmeal and dried fruit. After exchanging our previous night's dreams, we found that both had been nightmarish. It reminded me of being in the Himalayas at high altitudes when my dreams would vary between psychedelic and spooky. Jeff had dreamed of a "Freddy"-type monster chasing him up and down elevators in Boston.

My dream found me crawling out of our tent in the morning to find that through some transcendental witchcraft, we were in the midst of a hostile African tribe. I kept begging them that whatever method they had used to displace us from New Mexico to Africa was not funny and they should immediately conjure up the necessary potion to return us where we had been. Our tent was just sitting there right in the midst of these angry black tribesmen who were trying to figure out what to do with us.

We spread our bodies on the ponchos amidst the

moist grass under the hot sun. A nervous little chipmunk was about ten feet away trying to figure out how to get through the plastic ziplock bag into our peanuts.

Sitting in the lush green grass in the warmth of the sun, listening to the rushing water in the stream, hearing the wind blow through the aspen trees, and seeing the mountains all around in the shape of gigantic whales makes me realize that life certainly is perfect. It is true, like the book says, that there is perfection even in imperfection. Life is worth living and it makes me feel so lucky to have been given a life and to have the sheer pleasure of these moments to cherish. I feel sorry for those who have to live in a noisy, polluted city. It seems sad when people are so crowded together and there is no secret hiding place in nature to be alone with your thoughts. As for me, give me the wide open spaces where I am in the midst of a crowd of trees, grass, wild flowers, birds, mountains, and chipmunks who try to rip off my peanuts.

Do I get lonely? Ha! Quite the contrary; I feel most bored when I am with uninteresting people. But there is nothing tiresome about communicating with nature. I have learned to feel so much a part of it. There is a fine thread of energy that runs through all things. You can call it God or whatever word suits your fancy, but nevertheless there is a oneness in it all. Everyone of those plants, animals, and minerals are as communicative as people, if a person will just allow themselves to be sensitive enough to listen and hear what nature has to say.

There are travelers who come from large cities to our Hostel in the Forest merely looking for an inexpensive place to stay the night. They lock up their cars, want keys to secure their rooms, are afraid to walk the 100 feet from the parking lot to the Hostel, and would not be caught dead out on the hiking trails. I feel sorry for them and wish so much that they could stay around the Hostel long enough to acclimatize. It is necessary for people to get off the busy highways and away from the hustle and bustle and the rush of life. We deliberately leave the one-half mile entrance road to the Hostel bumpy with large enough holes to slow the cars down as they come off the interstate.

Maybe the wide open spaces of the Sangre de Cristo Mountains are not for everyone. But for me, it provides the tonic that I need to remind me who I really am. As Jeff and I stared into the solar system the night before and talked of galaxies five billion light years away, it made me starkly aware that I am an infinitesimal part of the whole thing. Like a cell of a human body, I am a similar portion of the whole thing. Each human is like that cell, but what we often forget is that those trees, streams, wildflowers, mountains, and animals are also kindred cells that are so necessary in making up the whole body. They are our spiritual brothers as well as our human counterparts and should be respected as such.

When a human dies, a new baby is born to take his place. Trees die and new seedlings are popping up all around. We all go through our evolutionary cycles. Jeff is keenly aware that I am the full-grown tree and he is the young sapling. We communicate as well together as those aspens blowing in the wind, but we both know that I have more rings around my trunk than he does. In not too many years, it will be his turn to teach his son about the ways of life. We have made a solemn vow that this will not be the last father-son venture into the world of nature and that he will pass all these thoughts and feelings into the minds of his children.

We had basked in the sun so long that we almost forgot that there was some ground to cover that day. The afternoon sun was going in and out of clouds. When the sun was out, it was hot. But when it hid itself behind a cloud, the temperature dropped considerably. If we had been carrying a thermometer, it would have constantly moved up and down like an elevator.

The trail we walked was almost level along a ridge covered with pale-barked aspens. It was an easy walk with magnificent views off to our left. We could see the bald Truchas Peak which stands at 13,100 feet. The trail we were walking was at 10,200 feet.

We met two pair of father-son teams from Santa Fe heading up for a Saturday night camp-out. The two young sons appeared to be about 12. What a great way to spend a weekend, both for the father and the son!

Later we met a couple of hikers in their twenties from Oklahoma City. They had hiked up to the top of Truchas Peak and were astounded at how two guys from Georgia could have ever found this place.

The trail descended to the convergence of the west fork and middle fork of the Santa Barbara River. We crossed the river by means of two decaying logs traversing the swift water. This can be a little tricky when carrying a 50-pound backpack. We then got off the trail to look for a campsite.

Jeff was walking ahead of me. All of a sudden, he jumped back into me. I looked down to see that he had almost stepped on a three-foot bull snake. We watched it slither off into the grass. From then on, we both caught ourselves spending more time looking downward than upward.

There were many good campsites along the

stream. We naturally chose one as close to the water as possible. The spaghetti had been saved for our Saturday night finale. It's not an easy feat to make food tasty on a backpacking trip, so I decided to go all out and pour all the seasonings together. The noodles cooked up very nicely on the little single-burner butane stove, and we had worked up a ravenous appetite. The combination of all the seasonings was considerably heavy with garlic powder and dried minced onion. In fact, it was so overpowering that Jeff commented, "I have to throw up the white flag on this." We had a good laugh and had to fill our bellies with the remaining bread and cheese.

The stars again lit up the sky for our last night together. We spread out the ponchos and put the sleeping mattresses on them to do a little gazing up into the heavens.

We laid there for hours talking about many things. First, I told stories of my growing up in Pineview and my first adventures at trying to camp out. He then confessed some of his mischievous doings as a child that I had never heard about before. We brought the evening to a close by expressing our love and respect for each other as sleep set in.

I am always the early riser. At home I rarely miss the sun emerging from the Atlantic Ocean. In the mountains, I can't actually see the sunrise like we do on the beach, but the soft glows light up the sides of the mountains and make a spectacular sight.

I kept thinking that this was the final day and I didn't want it to end. The cool, crisp morning air that made me pull out my down jacket would soon be replaced by the hot, muggy, and sultry conditions of southern Georgia in August. This communion with Jeff had been almost too perfect, but life must go on.

They say that you should never look back because there is no way to ever change the past. But if there was any way to turn back the hands of the clock, the one thing I would do is spend as much time as possible with my children. Giving material things to the children doesn't mean a thing, but I would want to give them more of me.

I was the type of person who was never absent from school a single day, the Mr. Conscientious type. That attitude has been with me always, so that I had to give 110 percent to my work, make as much money as I could, and support my family in a style that I felt like they deserved. I thought that I was being the sacrificial person. But now it all seems like such a cop out. Was I using the excuse of my family to satisfy my own ego? What could it possibly matter if I had gained the whole world, but lost the love and respect of my children?

As I sat there, I stared at a plant growing beside the stream, which was obviously the parent plant for a lot of seedlings growing all around underneath it. It appeared to be an annual that would die this fall when the snows come. The small plants would somehow suffer through the winter and then they would become the parent plant next summer. It's as true with us humans as it is in nature, that our greatest purpose in life is to reproduce. Everything else we do pales in comparison, and there is no better way to concentrate time and energy than spending it with your child.

There is no doubt that we must have money to live in this society. It has been my experience that the more I make, the more I spend, and my lifestyle continues to always stay one step ahead of my income. Perhaps the best way is to set standards for a simple lifestyle and make only enough money to meet the basic needs. This would then free us and give us more spare time to just live and enjoy life

The older I get, the more simple are my pleasures. It may be in a baby's smile, the twinkling of an eye, the loveliness of the wildflowers, a sunrise, or just sitting and talking to my child. All of these things cost only a little of my time and have turned out to be life's most magic moments.

We packed for the last leg of the hike descending to the Santa Barbara campground at 9200 feet. The vegetation was lush with dense groves of aspen and spruce and an occasional meadow thick with white daisies. The trail followed along the stream where fishermen were trying their luck on mountain trout.

We both felt some regret at seeing this adventure into fairyland end. It was not necessary to express to each other our awareness that something very special had transpired the last few days. We had gorged ourselves on the banquet that life has to offer, if one has the courage to reach out for it. Little did we know, however, that the banquet was going to be topped off with an exquisite dessert.

Dick and Robin met us at the campground and drove us to Ojo Caliente, an ancient hot mineral springs. Our tired bodies were soaked in the hot waters, which contain iron, sodium, arsenic, lithium, and other chemicals that reputedly have therapeutic value.

As we drove down the mountain, all aglow from the setting sun, I randomly sneaked a peek in the blue book for one last word of inspiration:

"The experiences of today make us a different person from whom we were yesterday."

How true it is.

DIE MAUER

CHAPTER FIVE

Photo: Klaus and Tom at Berlin Wall

C H A P T E R   5

DIE MAUER

In my years of travels, I have exchanged addresses with a multitude of people. The great majority of them are never remembered again. However, some have become friends, and we have not only written letters but have visited each other. One of the unforgettable names in my address book is Klaus Jahn from Rostock, Germany (formerly in East Germany/DDR).

It was the summer of 1973. I ventured into the communist world of Yugoslavia, Bulgaria, Romania, Hungary, and Czechoslovakia. It was a most exciting trip. I stayed in homes and learned a little about their customs and culture and how different they are from ours.

The Tatra Mountains separating Poland and Slovakia are especially good for hiking. Klaus, his wife Sigi, and their two young sons were completing a family hike when we met as we boarded the train. I was fascinated to talk with someone from the DDR and fortunately he could speak enough English for us to communicate. His two sons made me homesick, being about the same ages as mine. They were all excited to hear about life in America since I was the first American they had ever met.

I talked to Klaus about my family, my work, and some things about my country. He told me about his hometown of Rostock on the North Sea and his work in a fishing industry. He loved sports, especially mountain hiking, rock climbing, canoeing, kayaking, and Scuba diving. With his love for the outdoors, we obviously hit if off from the beginning.

He told of how the beaches in Rostock were patrolled by guards with machine guns. There was no swimming or use of any kind of floating device beyond 150 meters from the shore. If they did, the patrols from the towers would begin firing. Diving was prohibited in the sea since the government was afraid people would escape. So, Klaus was limited to diving only in lakes inside the country.

With tears in his eyes, he told me that his life-long dream was to go trekking in the Himalayas and diving in the Bahamas, but that possibility was very remote. At that time, he could only travel outside his country to Czechoslovakia and Poland. He was not allowed to visit other countries until after his 65th birthday and that would be possible only if he left his wife at home. At that age, he was afraid he would not want to trek and dive.

Life was not easy for Klaus. He refused to join the communist party. That meant no promotions at work, a very small apartment, a ten-year wait for a car, and many other disadvantages. When we talked of political things, we walked to the end of the train car away from other people; he was afraid someone would overhear what we were saying.

The train ride from Prague to East Berlin stopped at the DDR border. My first introduction to his country brought about a lot of hassles since I was an American. I was trying to tell them I only wanted a transit visa; I was going directly to West Berlin. I'm not sure what they were saying to me, but they were obviously nervous about dealing with an American.

I thought how ironic it was that the Russian Revolution in 1917 was for the purpose of overthrowing the *czars* who suppressed the people and kept them down. The successors to the revolutionaries had now become *czars* themselves. The oppressed became the oppressors.

In East Berlin we bid farewell. I really felt that I had made a friend, but was definitely ready to leave his country. The East Germans wanted another piece of my dignity when I crossed checkpoint Charlie into the West by strip-searching me before allowing passage through to West Berlin.

After returning home, Klaus and I exchanged letters. He wrote to me in German and I wrote to him in English. Three years later, in 1976, I wanted to take Marie to Germany where we would attempt to visit Klaus and Sigi in Rostock. We made it to the DDR border by train and a German man who spoke English helped us obtain our visas. We purchased the required amount of DDR marks for each day of our intended visit.

We found the country to be very industrial with smokestacks everywhere. After a change of trains in Leipzig, the birthplace of Wagner and other notable musicians, we arrived in Dresden about ten o'clock in the evening. Since this was the home of the famous porcelain china, Marie was eager to do a little shopping the next morning. We found a small hotel. When the man checking us in saw our U.S. passports, he really freaked out. The police were called and they ordered us out of the country by midnight or be arrested.

I argued and showed them our visas and DDR money. But they were armed to the teeth and demanded that we leave immediately. Marie and I literally ran to the station and took the first train leaving the country. A few hours later we found ourselves at the Polish border.

We were literally shoved off the train in the middle of the night, not knowing where we were or where we were going. Eventually, we made it to Warsaw, with a bitter taste in our mouths for the DDR. I learned later that all of the letters Klaus and I wrote to each other were opened by the government. The letter I had written telling of our intended visit was never received by him.

Seven years later in 1983, I made a visit to Berlin to visit some friends. I sent a telegram to Klaus, because like most of the DDR people, he didn't have a phone. Klaus arranged for us to meet in East Berlin, the city where we had said goodbye ten years earlier.

I brought them honey from my beehives and Hostel T-shirts. They brought me apples from their garden plot. We spent an enjoyable day together. They showed me the bombed-out areas of East Berlin, which was the main part of downtown Berlin before the war. We saw war museums and a few new buildings, but it was strikingly different from the thriving metropolis of West Berlin.

We talked of the hated wall around West Berlin built in 1961 to keep the East Germans home. The wall was more than just a barrier; it was a symbol of how suppressed people can become enslaved. But as Klaus said, "It's hard to have a revolution when the other side has all the guns." They had tried to revolt in 1953 when he was 15 years old. The revolu-

tion lasted only two days, and many of the protesters
were killed. So they helplessly watched the wall being built, knowing that there was nothing that could
be done.

Klaus wrote in 1988 that he had heard a rumor
that the DDR government had permitted some
people to visit the West on the special occasion of an
elderly relative. He wanted me to send him a certified
copy of my mother's birth certificate and perhaps he
could work some scheme to come to America for her
birthday. Unfortunately, my mother doesn't have a
birth certificate, although there is no doubt she was
born. They didn't bother about such things as that
in Pineview back in those days. So Klaus had to try
other avenues because he wanted to come to
America very badly.

The Germans, in my opinion, are very good
people, hard working, and obedient. Give them a
task and they take pride in doing it better than
anyone else. That may be an asset, but it may also
be their worst fault. Hitler made them believe in him,
and they followed him without questioning. After
World War II, Germany was divided into two countries. One half became the most productive capitalistic country in all of Europe and third in the entire
world. The other half became the best of all of the
eastern bloc communist countries. In many re-
spects, they were better communists than the Rus-
sians, another example of German determination.

Honecka was a suppressive head of state of the
DDR and he, along with many bureaucratic leaders,
became wealthy while the populace remained
obedient.

When Gorbechev began his policy of *Perestroika*,
some of the eastern bloc countries began to think

that maybe the time had come for the big break. It started with Lech Walesa and his solidarity movement in Poland. They ousted Jerulselski and formed a noncommunist government in August, 1989. That is when the movement to overthrow the communist dictatorship started in the churches of the DDR.

The two main German churches were Catholic and Lutheran. It was the Lutheran Church in Leipzig that started talk of revolt. I am sure Martin Luther, the founder of the Protestant Reformation, would have been proud that the seeds of protest were being planted in the church that bears his name. The movement then spread to the other churches. Leipzig is in the heart of Saxony, and Rostock lies in north of Mecklinberg. According to Klaus, Saxony seems to always be ahead of them, and thus their protest began two weeks later there.

When Gorbechev said he would not send the tanks to quell revolts the way they did in 1968 against the Czechs, that was the signal that Russian domination of these countries was dwindling. They saw the chance for self-determination.

On November 7, 1989, as the world watched, the Berlin Wall came down, and people from the DDR poured through to observe firsthand the fruits of capitalism. We all shared in their enthusiasm. It was not enough for me to watch it on television. I wanted to view it firsthand and try to make contact with Klaus.

I am lucky to have a wonderful wife who permits me to make spur-of-the-moment trips, and as a good travel agent, she gets me cheap flights. Ted accompanied me since he would be leaving after Christmas for two years in Jamaica with the Peace Corps, and this would give us a chance to have some time together. We decided to go on a Monday and left two days later on Wednesday.

Delta flies directly from Atlanta to Munich, and when we arrived, we were met by our good friend Heinz. He had a long weekend, so the three of us drove to Prague to see what the world had been watching on TV. Wincelas Square was filled with hundreds of thousands of demonstrators. It was exciting to participate in their brand new ability to protest without reprisal. When we left home, it was 75 degrees, but it was 5 above (F.) in Prague. But it's easy to forget the cold when surrounded by history in the making.

We felt so happy for the Czech people being able to do things that we take for granted like putting up protest signs, wearing small Czech flags in their lapels to identify themselves with the movement, and placing candles and flowers on the spots where students were clobbered with clubs two weeks earlier. All stood in the bitter cold without thought of the weather; fires of passion burned within.

Heinz drove us to Berlin to observe the fall of the Wall and participate with the many tourists in chiseling away at the mammoth structure. The DDR soldiers peered through the cracks in the wall with smiles on their faces. They walked on top of it and gladly posed for the Sunday afternoon photographers. How different it was when I was there in 1973 and 1983. It was very scary then, and there was fear to even go near the wall. We walked to the Potsdammer Platz where a section of the monstrosity had been removed, allowing cars and pedestrians to go back and forth. It was such an emotional feeling to see the ecstatic faces of the people pouring through the "crack in the wall."

We sent Klaus a telegram; within hours he took a train and made his first trip to West Berlin since the wall was erected in 1961. It was an emotional and tearful reunion for both of us. It was hard for him to express his feelings about being on the west side of the wall. He was filled with so much emotion, and I was, too.

We walked together down to the Brandenburg Gates, the entry into old Berlin. The wall sits only a few feet away from it. Berlin had special significance for him; both his mother and father were born in the Charlottenburg area of what is now West Berlin. It is sad that they didn't live to participate in this happy occasion.

Klaus stood for a long time speechless, staring at the west side of that dreadful structure. He broke the silence by telling me he felt very ashamed that his people were responsible for building it. What could I say? I also felt shame for anybody who had anything to do with it.

A few weeks earlier when many young people were leaving the DDR through the West German Embassy in Prague, both of his sons came to him. The older was 27, married, and had one child. The other son was 23 and unmarried. They asked their father's permission to leave.

Both Klaus and Sigi said, "Go, you must go."

They did and both of them had been in West Germany for a month. They found employment and planned to remain there.

Both of Sigi's parents were old and lived near Rostock, so Klaus and Sigi felt compelled to remain at home. Furthermore, Klaus said he wanted to be there to help clean up the political mess that had existed for over forty years. They really had no desire to leave their home, but they wanted freedom to travel, freedom to elect their government, and freedom from the domination of the communist party.

Klaus was proud that he kept his dignity and refused to ever join the party. He may not have had much money or a lot of material things, but he had self-respect.

He told me that in the past few weeks the churches had been filled with people giving thanks for what was happening. On December 2, the entire country took part in forming a giant human cross. One chain, consisted of 600,000 people holding hands, stretching the 600 kilometers from the North Sea to the Czech border. Many other hundreds of thousands held hands from the east border to the west. Wouldn't that have been a magnificent sight to look down upon from a satellite? Angels in heaven must have been smiling, too.

Klaus and Sigi made a trip to Georgia for a visit in the spring of 1990. His dreams were beginning to come true, and it made me very happy to be a small part of it. The DDR people are good and "you can't keep good people down;" at least, not very long. They were coming back. The opinion was divided about a reunification with West Germany or remaining a separate country. Klaus favored reunification. Who knows what will be best? It was all happening so fast there wasn't time to digest it.

Klaus and I had stood by the wall as long as we could. Then both of us rushed over and borrowed a hammer and chisel from a determined tourist trying to get a souvenir. We smashed that damned wall as hard as we could. Little slithers of it flew everywhere as we pounded. Poor Klaus even skinned his thumb, but the pain was numbed by his enthusiasm.

We then walked together over to a billboard that had just been erected and read it together:

DIE MAUER (THE WALL)

"The wall is crumbling. It was the symbol of a battle between two systems. We thank all friends from the German Democratic Republic and the Federal Republic of Germany who have now left this struggle behind.

"In our own country, a joy has arisen in which we all partake. This joy comes from the feeling of a universal human sense of belonging rather than from the triumph of victory. No one has won yet, for we will only have won when all systems and all walls have been overcome. No one will be able to find the human happiness that we all long for by changing from one system to another. The question of human freedom lies outside all existing political systems. It has not been resolved on either side. The West has more glitter, more drive, and more riches, but it too has no real answers to the hopes with which hundreds of thousands are now coming to us after having lived behind the walls for so long.

"At this moment, we thank the New Forum of the DDR for their earnest reflections.

"We have always built walls. We have built them to protect ourselves. They have been built around peoples, around political systems, and around religious beliefs. They have been built around elementary human concerns; around Eros, love, and partnership. Every bit of insight, every bit of truth, and every bit of love that could be found in this difficult world was immediately protected by a wall, an ideology, or a law. To the outside world, this was a demonstration of strength, but at the same time it was always a protection against fear.

"But the freedom we all long for is without fear. It is founded on an understanding and solidarity common to all, on friendship and truth between people, who no longer have to build walls to protect themselves. Wherever walls are needed to protect truth, humaneness, and freedom against the world, we have contradiction. For human beings can only be truly free in this world if they no longer need barriers or walls. Faithfulness to a *system*, meaning more than just paying lip service, can only arise when other systems are understood and recognized, too. This is equally true for politics as it is for love:

> You can only be faithful
> if you are allowed to love others, too.

"Maybe a part of the Berlin Wall should remain standing as a reminder of a human error to which we all contributed. We could paint both sides of it with the expression of our will to overcome such walls for all times. Berlin would then again be a spiritual capital in a new sense, a metropolis and a symbol for new, humane, and political thinking in the sense of *Glasnost* and *Perestroika* and in the sense of human friendship — in the name of warmth for everything that wants to live in the future."

KILIMANJARO —
MARIE'S TRIUMPH

C H A P T E R   S I X

Photo: Stephen, Marie and Tom atop Kilimanjaro

CHAPTER 6

KILIMANJARO — MARIE'S TRIUMPH

The excitement and anticipation of climbing to the summit of that dormant volcano known as Kilimanjaro and the constant roar of the jumbo 747 kept sleep at bay somewhat like overzealous guard dogs.

Tourist class seats on an airplane are obviously designed by some maniacal sadist; no amount of twisting and turning resulted in a position of comfort. A baby cried nearby and my body joined in chorus. In fact, my entire being was pleading for mercy on this 30-hour marathon from St. Simons Island, Georgia, to Nairobi, Kenya.

Layovers in New York and London offered little relief. Truthfully, fatigue had set in before leaving home. Late nights of attempting to get the work load in some reasonable fashion and desperately watching every moment of the Braves' struggle for a spot in the World Series had me strung out prior to setting foot on a plane.

As the packed aircraft crossed over the greyish-blue Mediterranean, the cumulous clouds parted for a bird's-eye view of the vast Sahara Desert with its giant sand dunes interrupted only by the flow of the River

Nile. The setting sun cast a reddish glow over the Earth's most forbidding territory stretching on and on in its desolation into equatorial Africa.

I reached for the hand of my wife to receive a bit of caress and reassurance. But Marie slept like there was no tomorrow. It is amazing how she can fit sleep into such adverse circumstances. Neither a lightning storm nor a Van Halen concert could bring her back into reality.

A call for a medical doctor on board brought forth an emergence of five passengers claiming that special qualification. They awkwardly attended a young woman who had lost consciousness. This heaped coals on my disquietment. There seemed to be real concern that they could not revive her lifeless body. Fortunately for both of us, we soon touched ground in balmy Nairobi. The patient came back to life, and I was re-prieved from the seat of torture which imprisoned me.

Every former British colony seems to specialize in some sort of nightmarish bureaucratic maze. There are meaningless forms to be completed and many long lines that always test the patience of those who are accustomed to American efficiency. We were greeted with the horrifying pronouncement that all travelers fear and loathe. Our bags were not on the flight. The approach of midnight on our life-less bodies and the extended consolation that an-other plane would be coming in two days was a bit unnerving. But our experience in travel permitted us to remain unperturbed.

The 18-kilometer ride from the airport to the city center seemed short. Our conversant cab driver was a tea farmer during the week and jockied a white Mercedes on weekends to pick up a few extra shil-lings for his four wives and 13 kids. I was awed by his tenacity and certainly paled in comparison, but actually, one wife and three children seemed to be quite enough for me.

When my body finally found a prone position in a hotel bed, the snoring man in the adjacent room was no match for me. I literally died until the blowing horns of morning traffic brought me back into reality.

It was Kenyatta Day for all of Kenya to celebrate this patriot who led the fight for their independence from the stronghold of British colonialism. All shops and businesses seemed to observe this special holiday, and we found nothing open but a movie house with two theaters. One appeared to be an X-rated flick called *Party Line*. We chose the other as being more fitting, *In The Shadow Of Kilimanjaro*. The price was right at $1.25, and the tasty popcorn was only 50 cents a box. Our tickets designated a seat number obliging us to occupy that particular one because every ticket was sold.

After standing for the playing of their national anthem, while viewing the waving flag of Kenya on the screen, we settled down for the newsreel, a series of commercials, and finally the main feature. During this period, hawkers walked up and down the aisles selling pop, soda, and juices.

The movie starred a reputable American actor, Timothy Bottoms, but the film left a lot to be desired. Furthermore, it was extremely disconcerting to see a purported true story of baboons terrorizing villages and devouring people during the drought of 1984. It was especially bothersome since it occurred in the area where we planned to hike. Marie and I both agreed that if we saw one baboon on the trail, we were out of there.

Nairobi is a thriving, bustling city of 1.5 million

people, filled with skyscrapers and new construction going on all about. It is exceptionally clean and attempts to be very European with fine hotels, restaurants, and coffee shops. If a world conference or convention of some sort is to be held in Africa, it would be in Nairobi. It tries to portray itself as the capital of the continent.

Our milk-white appearance obviously called attention to us as we walked along the sidewalks in a sea of black faces. But we found all of the people to be extremely nice and helpful.

Needless to say, we were tired of wearing the same clothes for the fourth straight day. The call from the airport that our bags had arrived was greeted with about the same enthusiasm that we would have accorded the Braves winning the World Series or Santa Claus arriving on Christmas morning.

Dressed in fresh clothes, we struck out to the market place on Muindi Mbingu Street where there are some excellent buys in all manner of African sisal handbags, handcarved ebony, jewelry, and most anything a souvenir hunter would want. Our day ended at a restaurant with the finest of taste called Foresta Magnetica, one block from the Hilton Hotel. Another recommendation for the lover of Indian cuisine was Manir, where the next night we enjoyed as good a curry as I have ever tasted for less than $10 for both of us.

Excitement was mounting to a high pitch when we boarded the 35-minute flight from Nairobi to the Kilimanjaro Airport in Tanzania. The pilot flew so close to the top of the mountain that I felt I could reach out and touch this highest peak on the African continent.

From the airport, we rode for about an hour

through small villages to the Kibo Hotel at the base of the mountain near the tribal village of Marangu. Mr. Dilly, a nice man from the State Travel Agency in Arusha had arranged the hike. He was standing by to meet us when we arrived.

Tanzania has hundreds of tribes. Each one has its own dialect distinguishable from the others. The one common language binding them all together is Swahili which they learn in school. At the hotel, Mr. Dilly joined us for a lunch consisting of a good tasty soup, broiled chicken, French fries, tomatoes garnished with sliced bell peppers, cabbage, carrots, a cold Safari beer, and followed by a delicious bread pudding. I was astounded to pick up the bill for all three of us, and including the tip, it came to a whopping $3.75.

All of the natives we met were almost childlike in their graciousness and politeness. Everyone we met gave us the familiar greeting, *Jambo* (meaning "Hello"), *Habari* ("How are you?"), and *Missouri* ("Just fine."). The smallest child to the oldest adult exchanges this dialogue with everyone they meet. The genuine smiles on their charblack faces expose pearly white teeth making all strangers feel comfortable and welcome. Peaceful, contented, and happy are adjectives I would use to describe these people.

Families live in huts surrounded by a jungle of banana trees. Rows of coffee plants are raised under the large banana leaves. Beans, tomatoes, peppers, potatoes, peas, yams, and ginger grow in the gardens. Some of the men frequent the local bars where banana beer is sold, which we were told was very strong and a bit expensive (about $1.50). Little children ran up to us and politely held out their hands, saying, "Sweets, sweets." We felt sorry we didn't bring anything to give them.

The Kibo Hotel not only serves generous help-
ings of good, inexpensive food, but also rents any
kind of hiking clothes or equipment that one might
need. We acquired sleeping bags, sweaters, ponchos,
and walking sticks.

The bells of the nearby Lutheran Church wake
everyone within a country mile at 6:00 a.m. sharp.
The excitement of the upcoming hike put butterflies
in our stomachs, so there was no going back to sleep.

The hotel sits at about 5500 feet altitude. Our
first day's hike was up to a campsite called Mandara
at 9000 feet that has several A-frame huts with
comfortable beds and solar-powered lighting. The
$169 entrance fee into the national park permits
them to maintain all of the campsites in excellent
condition.

After leaving the park entrance, the trail proceeded up a well-worn path lush with ferns, large
vines of flowering plants, streams of crystal-clear
water, and jungle-like noises where monkeys occasionally ran across the path in front of us. Our
guide, Zakaria, and his assistant, Stephen, had four
porters accompany them. Their duties were to carry
all the food, equipment, and our gear, all securely
balanced on the tops of their heads. It made the
carrying of our small daypacks seem woefully inad-
equate in comparison.

A drizzle of rain peppered down on the tin roof as
we sat in the dining hall at Mandara Hut munching
on soup, beef, potatoes, carrots, cabbage, slaw, and
hot tea. Other groups of hiking parties were seated
around tables exchanging experiences. There were
Germans, Austrians, British, New Zealanders, French-
men, and one American from San Francisco. We
could distinguish where we were to sit by the color of

table cloths. Ours was red-and-white checkered.

A clearing at sunset produced a magnificent rainbow. I walked outside with Zakaria, and we talked about many things. Being modern in his outlook, he has only one wife and one child. As the oldest son, he was expected to care for his aging mother after the death of his father a few years previously.

"Just how old is your mother?" I asked.

"Oh, she's 57," he answered reverently, as if she were ancient.

From that moment, I tried to avoid any questions about age. I was afraid he might think I was too old to go up the mountain.

His fervent wish was to someday buy a small plot of land to build his own little hut for his family because under tribal law everything his mother owned would go to the youngest son upon her death. It was not easy for them to make much money. For this five-day hike, he would be paid a total of $20 and the porters $10. An apprenticeship of several years was required before one could become a guide, including a good knowledge of rope climbing. If his clients wanted to go up on another side of the mountain, it required technical climbing. His use of English was surprisingly good, and we chatted at length.

"Tom, what is it like in America for black people?" he asked.

This was not an easy question to answer and required some pondering on my part. I had just seen the movie, *Boyz In The Hood*, portraying the struggle for blacks living with drugs and violence in Los Angeles. This sort of thing did not exist in this part of Africa. The crime in the ghettos of American cities was not something that they have any knowledge about.

The children in their school uniforms attended

classes without any discipline problems. While they had no electricity or modern conveniences, everyone seemed to be happy and contented, which was not something I could say about most Americans. The "medicine man," or herbal doctor as they are now called, dispensed roots, herbs, and teas made from tree bark which seemed to take care of most of their maladies.

Finally, I said, "Zakaria, you may not know it, but there are a lot of poor people in America."

He looked at me as if to say with tongue in cheek, "Sure there are."

"I figure that the richest man is the one with the fewest worries and has peace of mind," I continued. "Most often the person who has a lot of material things has more stress and worries. It seems to me that you may be the richest man that I have met in a long time."

He laughed.

Here our conversation was interrupted by a leopard that entered the grounds about 50 feet away from us. It wandered about searching for any bits of food left by campers. My wife made a vow not to visit the restroom on this dark night without my going with her, although I'm not very experienced in leopard fighting.

In the morning, after a hearty breakfast of toast, a hard-boiled egg, and a bowl of hot cream of wheat, we set out on a six-hour hike up to the Horombu Huts located at 12,000 feet. The trail meandered over a grassy plain they refer to as a *savannah*, but is what I call wire grass. Mount Kilimanjaro loomed to the left and the mountain of Mawenzi towered on the right. The mist which fell the night before at Mandara was instead a heavy snow on the mountaintops, giving them a clean and sparkling appearance.

Our companions along the path were Rob and Hillery, a couple from New Zealand. She was a medical doctor and had been doing volunteer work in a West African hospital where they had experienced a cholera epidemic. He was a land surveyor and had volunteered through an interdenominational Christian organization to help build a water system in Ethiopia.

The A-frame huts at Horombu sit at 12,000 feet, high up on a hill, normally providing a great view of both mountains. But on our arrival the area was enshrouded in a thick fog. The weather was a bit windy and chilly — about 40 degrees, I would guess. Our porters, who had ventured on ahead, greeted us with a pot of hot tea that was pretty tasty. Several brave but friendly mice ran around on the floor of the dining hall looking for a morsel that some clumsy hiker might have left.

That night we had to share our small hut with a German man who had come down from the top of Kilimanjaro. He had little to say about his trials and tribulations, but we didn't want to hear any bad stories at this point. Being a typical Bavarian, he downed a couple of beers before crawling into the sleeping bag for a well-deserved rest.

The higher the altitude, the less one can sleep. Long nights are filled with restless rolling and tossing. The mind plays foolish tricks because any dreaming always falls into the category of being weird. Finally, morning triumphantly marched in to rescue the disquieted souls from the horrors of the night. Our down jackets and hoods were pulled out of the bags for the first time to protect against the wind and cold that snuck in and paid us a visit before sunrise. The *diamox* we were taking to ward off altitude sickness had worked for me. But Marie's stomach felt a bit queasy. Fruit was the only nourishment she could force down while I ate heartily of toast, butter, and jam without hesitation.

The walk through "the desert" to the next hut gains 3500 feet in altitude. It is above the tree line so no greenery or savannahs line the path. It appeared as though we were walking on the moon. The trail ascends gradually so even though we spent seven hours of trudging along, it was not a tongue-dragger. The scenery is not one that compels constant picture taking once you have taken your fill of the towering two mountains of Mawenzi and Kilimanjaro.

Mawenzi is jagged with spires and fortifications that make it appear as a giant fortress while Kilimanjaro looks like a vanilla ice cream cone.

The long hike gave us much time to share our thoughts. Although Marie had hiked with me on the Appalachian Trail many times, this was really her first one where extreme difficulties were to be experienced. She had never encountered a tough climb at high altitudes.

"This is not a trip that I can sell to any of my clients in the travel business," she lamented wearily. "They want plush accommodations and everything made easy."

This brought on my dissertation, which she, of course, now knows by heart, of how one day America was a great country because it was filled with adventurers who had a frontier spirit. The people who descended on the wide-open spaces of our new country didn't mind roughing it and suffering through hardships to carve out a place where there were freedoms from oppression. They had a zeal, a motivation, a drive, a hearty spirit, and were not

View of Kilimanjaro from Horombu Hut (12,000 ft.).

afraid to work hard for what they believed in.

Today, our country has developed a large population of spoiled brats. We have it much too easy and complain bitterly if something is too hard. Where our ancestors built their houses and lived their lives by the sweat of their brows, we flick a switch to get most things that we want. Frankly, I'm not sure that this makes us better people. If anything goes wrong that requires us to endure any type of hardship, not only do we gripe and bitch, but we want to sue whoever might have caused us to undergo such difficulties. The old frontier spirit has been lost. No longer is a handshake between two people sufficient. It now requires reams of legal documents to try to hold them to their word.

We are a bunch of softies who spend most of our lives trying to feather our nests to make ourselves more comfortable. While I confess to being a member of this new breed of oafs, I found that my trek up to Mount Everest set a new standard for me by which to measure things. If I am walking up a long flight of stairs, and it seems a little hard, I always think back to what I was able to accomplish physically on that trip, and somehow my mental attitude kicks into overdrive. What seemed to be hard is somehow made easier. I told Marie that this hike would do the same for her.

The porters were happy to see us arrive around 3:00 p.m. and immediately brought hot tea to warm the tired bodies. The Kibo Hut sits at 15,500 feet, and the sun had already begun its descent behind the mountain. This was the usual signal to pull out our warmest clothes, and we scampered for ours immediately.

It seemed to be an ideal time to use some of the dehydrated foods we brought with us and took as our first choice the turkey tetrazzini. Water had to be carried on some poor porter's head from Horombu Hut since there was no water at Kibo Hut. Zakaria boiled some for us which brought the dried food to life and made it palatable. In pulling out our warmest clothes to get ready for the final ascent, Marie and I made occasional inquiring glances at each other. Finally, the silence was broken.

"What do you think?" I asked.

"I don't know," was her only reply.

"Are you going to try it?"

"I'll try," she answered doubtfully.

"Look, we don't have to kill ourselves to prove anything."

She agreed.

"But I came this far and I don't want to turn

back now."

"I'll start out," Marie replied, "but if I see I can't make it, I'm turning back."

"That's okay. That's what you should do. Both Zakaria and Stephen are going with us, so if one of us gets sick, there will be a guide to come down."

"Yes, I know." She was still undecided.

"Look, I may be the one who gets sick, and if I have to come down, I want you to keep going. Let's at least try to get one of us to the top."

That suggestion was met by silence, but having lived with this woman for almost 30 years, I know that she is cut out of a tough piece of cloth. We crawled into our sleeping bags and pulled sheets of plastic over them to help hold in the heat. It was only 6:00 p.m. but Zakaria had promised to awake us at midnight to start our ascent so we needed to try to get a few hours of sleep.

I can't remember if I ever lost consciousness, but that fateful tap, tap, tap on the door came precisely at the witching hour. A stone had been placed against the door to prevent the winds from blowing it open. By this time, we had come to love Zakaria, who was always so attentive to our needs, although this was not a visit from him that we particularly relished.

He held a peace offering with a cup of hot tea in each hand. That was enough to bring us both to the sitting position. He smiled as he served each of us in bed. The solar light was illumined and revealed a message carved on the side of my bed:

"After enduring this, I decided to
take up scuba diving."

Our laughter temporarily broke the spell of fright that had enveloped both of us. We knew that it would be the hardest and most physically demanding thing either of us had ever done. The process of layering the clothing on our bodies began: two pair of wool socks beneath our hiking boots; undergarments, long-johns, jeans, and rain pants to protect us from the waist down; a T-shirt, long-john pullover, cotton shirt, wool sweater, and down jacket for the upper body; and a wool scarf, nylon head liner, wool sock-hat, and down hood over that. The reports from the previous night had estimated minus 20 degrees centigrade at the top.

We stepped outside in what seemed like suits of armor that should have been quite sufficient to keep us warm. Three men who stayed in the room across from us were bent over double heaving their guts out. There was nothing but sympathy from me because I well remembered my altitude sickness in the Himalayas a few years back. The moon was only two nights past full, shining brightly to light our way and making headlamps a useless bit of gear.

Zakaria looked at me as if to say, "Is Marie going?"

I nodded. We both doubted that she had the conviction necessary to successfully reach the peak. It is 4,000 feet straight up, and one has to want to do it very badly to endure what it dishes out.

The weather was bone-chilling, but the gods smiled on us — there was no debilitating wind. The four of us pressed upward using our African oak walking sticks on each step.

Zakaria set a slow pace, and Marie followed making sure she placed her foot exactly where he did. As the third in line, I trudged along acting as a cheerleader for my wife, and Stephen represented the caboose of our train. Not a sound could be heard. The silence was only broken by the pressure of our boots on the frozen ground and the constant jabs of our walking sticks. The trail zigzagged up the mountain, strewn with lava rock and dust. Pebbles filled the pathway that made it somewhat like walking on marbles. Zakaria continually reminded us, "Polé, polé" (slowly, slowly).

I expressed words of encouragement to Marie, who in turn gave me a psychological boost as well. The four of us edged upward on the switchbacks at a snail's pace. When one gets above 15,000 feet, the lack of oxygen plays a significant role in making even the slightest movements tiring. Every few steps, we stopped to rest. Each of us carried a quart of water in our canteens and a sack of gorp for an infusion of energy.

The snow on the summit appeared so close, teasing us into believing that it was easily within our grasp. Looking back at Kibo Hut, it became smaller and smaller as we distanced ourselves from it. Around 4:00 a.m., we arrived at Hans Meyer Cave at 17,000 feet. It was named for the first person to climb to Kilimanjaro's summit. Zakaria assured us that this was the halfway point.

"It couldn't be," I argued. "Look back at how far we've come and the top of the mountain is just right there."

Zakaria tried to explain that what I was seeing was only an illusion and in fact the cave was half the distance to the top. I was not convinced that my eyes would play that kind of trick on me, but of course, in time he was proven right, and I was dead wrong.

Marie still pushed forward and amazingly enough did not give up after our short rest in the cave.

By 5:00 a.m., the weather turned significantly colder. We climbed continually upward in order to keep warm. Joyously, it seemed that the proverbial snows of Kilimanjaro might be within our grasp. The last few hundred yards the trail became much steeper.

Marie had her eyes glued to Zakaria's feet in front of her so as not to make a misstep. By this time, Zakaria held her by the hand, pulling her from one large boulder to another while I pushed from behind. She was absolutely petrified to look down, claiming to be afraid of heights. That was pretty laughable. As we reached 19,000 feet, the grade became even steeper. The test was grueling. It was a matter of digging way down deep inside to find that something extra to give. Our oxygen-starved bodies were screaming for a respite from such an ordeal.

"Just keep praying with every step you take," I reminded her. "Ask the Lord for extra strength."

"I haven't stopped praying since we left the Kibo Hut," she chided me.

This crazy mountain played head games with us. Every time it would seem that we were almost there, after another half hour of trudging upward it would appear to be further away. The oxygen-deprived brain doesn't always function properly. Its judgment is impaired.

We passed through a spot called Jamaica where a boy from that country had fallen to his death. It was also disconcerting to see a cross marking the spot where a German hiker died from altitude sickness (pulmonary edema). There was every good reason in the world to turn back except our stalwart determination (sometimes referred to as a hard

Marie and Zakaria approaching the summit.

View of the top of Kilimanjaro from our departing plane.

head) that urged us on to finish the goal.

Our steps at this point were no further than six inches apart. "Polé, polé," Zakaria repeated like a mantra.

There was really no need for this admonition since we were already trudging along at a slow pace. I explained to him our children's fable about the tortoise and the hare. "We're slow but sure."

We both laughed and continued to push upward toward our goal, the summit known as Gilmans Point, at 19,340 feet.

A little after six o'clock, the horizon began to glow with a reddish hue signaling the sunrise. Gradually, it became lighter. Then, in all of its glory on this beautiful Sunday morning, that big red ball peeped up dead-center of Mount Mawenzi. What a spectacle! It appeared as a glowing torch sitting atop that fortress-like castle. At the same time, the almost full moon was descending along the top of Kilimanjaro. Two powerful celestial bodies sandwiched us poor miserable mortals in between them creating that extra bit of energy we sorely needed.

With the constant encouragement of Zakaria and Stephen, we remained undaunted. The struggle paid off and finally by the grace of God, we both touched the metal cross marking the summit at 8:00 a.m., giving us the sensation of finding the pot of gold at the end of the rainbow. After scribbling our autographs in the book of those lucky few, Marie literally passed out beside the cross while I danced about getting sufficient photographs to prove that we really did it.

A large crater adorning this famous volcano is dotted with glaciers and snow and surrounded by a spiked crown. One could walk around the perimeter of it if there was any energy to spare. Zakaria told of a couple of Germans who insisted on pitching their tent and sleeping the night inside the crater. He laughed, "I do whatever the client wants to do if it's not too life-threatening."

But we were elated and quite satisfied with our own achievements. There was no time for me to triumph in my glory because all of my emotions flowed to my wife for having the intestinal fortitude and tenacity to stick with it to the bitter end. I was so proud of her success and gained a new respect and admiration for her abilities as a mountain-climbing companion that I had much too often overlooked in the past.

THE LUO AND THE MASAI

Photo: Masai woman.

CHAPTER 7

THE LUO AND THE MASAI

A trip to Africa wouldn't be complete without viewing all of the wild animals that have occupied the continent for centuries. A multitude of national parks have been established to protect them from hunters and poachers. One of the more popular ones is known as the Masai Mara National Reserve in the southwest of Kenya. It is a part of the Great Rift Valley, a fault in the Earth's surface that runs all the way from Turkey through the Middle East and down to South Africa. Another portion of this gigantic indentation is the Serengeti Plain in Tanzania which adjoins the Masai Mara on the south.

There are numerous "camps" within the reserves that provide game viewing excursions at least twice a day. Actually, they are rather plush accommodations where each one tries to outdo the other with arrays of culinary delights, fancy swimming pools, hot-air balloon rides, and elaborate land-scaping of native flowers and shrubs. They are vying for the much sought-after tourist dollar but do give a substantial amount of employment to people from neighboring tribes.

At a place called Kichwa Tembo, meaning elephant head, I became acquainted with two natives who made a lasting impression on me. Our long conversations and time spent together were highlights of the whole trip. Although they worked side by side for the camp, historically their tribes were bitter enemies. Both stoutly defended the way of life of their forefathers. The relationship between these two men, while polite on the surface, was obviously infected by wounds that had existed for centuries. Steven was a Luo and Linus belonged to that nomadic tribe of Masais. Feelings run deep because there is still a great deal of loyalty to their ancestors' way of life. What a character study to watch unfold right before my eyes!

"They are a bunch of thieves and cattle-stealers," was Steven's analysis of a typical Masai.

"Why do you say that?" I was surprised by his provocative remark.

"They killed my father's brother . . . stole all of his cows while he was out watching over them. I don't have no use for them."

There were Masai villages along the dirt trails leading into the game reserve. This heightened my enthusiasm to visit one of them. The mud huts were in a circle surrounded by a fence made of sticks and branches. One gate provided an entrance into the compound not only for the citizens of the village but also their farm animals for protection against carnivorous wildlife such as lions, leopards, cheetahs, hyenas, and wild dogs. The tribal chief was authorized by ancient tradition to determine when it was time to abandon the village and move on to greener pastures. Their entire lifestyle seemed to center around their cows, goats, sheep, and donkeys. The newborn animals even sleep inside their huts with them for the first few weeks of life.

"But how do I go about getting into one of these villages?" I wondered aloud. The tribesmen were reticent about strangers and spurned the taking of photographs for fear that it took away a part of their spirits or souls.

I was elated to meet Linus, a full-blooded Masai. He was a naturalist at Kichwa Tembo, Abercrombie and Kent's prize location near the site of the movie, *Out Of Africa*. Although quite conversant on all of the plant life in the area, I found him much more adept and enthusiastic about Masai life and traditions. With all of the skills that could be mustered in the art of cross-examination, I proceeded to milk from him as much information as he was willing to give.

"I was born a Masai and I will die a Masai," he boasted. "I am proud of my people. For as long as anyone knows, they have roamed these lands in search of the ideal spots for their animals. The Earth is sacred to them, and you will never find them scarring the soil in any way. We don't even bury our dead for fear of disturbing the Earth. The bodies are laid out on the plains for the animals to consume."

I was awed by his reverence for the land until my balloon was burst by Steven, the Luo, in a later conversation.

"Of course, they don't plant anything in the dirt because they are too lazy." Steven said. "You'll never find a Masai out digging and working like my people. We raise vegetables of all kinds, eat meat and fish. Masais never put anything in their mouths except milk and blood."

To my dismay, that evening Linus confirmed that their diet only consisted of the milk from cows and goats along with the blood that was drained from the jugular vein of their cattle.

Steven boasted that his people were known throughout the lands as fishermen. Anywhere there was a body of water, you'd find a tribe of Luos. "We eat fish every day," he bragged.

"You are a man after my own heart," I responded, being the fish lover in the family.

He told me how as a small boy he and his father used to fish very often in Lake Victoria aboard their homemade dugout canoe. "We always caught Nile perch. Most of the time, they would weigh between 50 and 100 pounds. Man, some of those fish were so big, we didn't even want to catch them. My father would say, 'Don't catch no fish bigger than the canoe.' You had to be careful 'cause if you tried to take the hook out of one of those big mouths, it would bite your hand right off. There's been many a time that we would find watches and rings in their stomachs."

I don't know whether to vouch for the veracity of this statement or just assume that fisherman are liars all over the world. But anyway it makes a good story.

"Eating fish is good for you," The big Luo swelled his body to expose its six-foot four-inch frame. "Both my daddy and my grandmother were taller than me. People used to think, when they saw that big woman coming over the hill, that she was a giant."

I'll have to admit that he was a healthy-looking specimen. His body was well filled out compared to the thin willowy appearance of the Masais. As a driver of one of the Toyota Land Cruisers, he was a whiz at finding and identifying animals and bird life. No matter what the terrain was like, he would throw on the four-wheel drive and go bouncing across it full speed ahead in search of a pride of lions or a den of hyenas.

We parked down by a river for a close-up view of a family of hippos being closely scrutinized by several fierce-looking crocodiles. Steven seemed to know all about the traits and habits of wildlife, but his great big eyes grew even larger when I told him my hippopotamus stories.

A few nights earlier at the Lake Naivasha Country Club, we enjoyed a sunset cruise to watch thousands of waterfowl gliding in for a few snacks before dark. Colorful flamingos, egrets, storks, herons, and a multitude of other varieties adorned the lake, causing much excitement among the ornithologists in our group. As we docked, an enormous hippo surfaced and wandered up to the beautifully landscaped grounds of the hotel to munch on the grass. Apparently, there was nothing unusual about that, but later a group of dogs started barking at this oversized monstrosity and chased him right smack into the swimming pool.

Well, this caused quite a stir among the hotel personnel. Everyone came out to see this phenomenon because no one had ever heard of a hippopotamus in a swimming pool. Furthermore, no one had any remote idea how they were going to get it out. Without a doubt, it became an overnight sensation and certainly the most photographed hippo in all of Africa. The next morning as we were leaving, game officials had arrived from Nairobi to figure out how to remove this five-ton hunk from its newfound captivity.

My other hippopotamus story came from one of the hikers we met in our climb up Kilimanjaro the week before. He had just returned from a trip to Mozambique. During his stay there, he booked a white-water canoe trip down the Zambesi River. There were three canoes of adventuresome tourists, packed with all their gear, paddling alongside scatterings of hippos and crocodiles, which was a bit unnerving in itself. Without any warning or provocation, an enormous hippo swam under the second canoe and flipped it upside down like it was a toy. As the terrified passengers struggled for shore, the bad-tempered beast bit the canoe right in half. Luckily, my friend was in the first canoe, but he said there was a lot of praying done for the remaining hours of the trip down the river.

Steven reckoned that no one but a fool would go in the water with hippos and crocodiles. He said a crocodile is a fast runner on the shore and can knock a person down with its tail before he would know what hit him.

As I said previously, each tribe speaks its own dialect totally different from the languages of other tribes. They are all taught Swahili in school so that they can communicate with each other, and their third language is English in order to speak to the white man. Being an American, it still amazed me to meet people with very little formal education who spoke three languages fluently. At home, we are all still struggling with just one.

At Kichwa Tembo, the guests sleep in tents that are a far cry from any tent that I have ever slept in. A wooden floor, twin beds, a bathroom with a flush toilet, and a hot shower are not exactly what I would call roughing it. On checking in, the patrons are introduced to the Baboon Chaser, a young Masai wrapped in his scarlet cloth garment designed to scare the animals away. The camp is surrounded by an electric fence that purportedly keeps the larger creatures out, although I'm sure any elephant that took a notion could walk right through it.

The first evening, while dining on the scrumptious array of foods, the Baboon Chaser was obviously asleep on the job. Our tent was invaded by one or more of the pesky creatures who proceeded to devour the entire basket of complimentary fruit and had a party in the middle of my bed. Everything had been thrown out of my suitcase and the ziplock plastic bags had been ripped up in a futile attempt to find other delectable edibles. The hotel personnel were very apologetic, but that didn't keep me from sleeping with one eye open the rest of the night in fear that the baboon might return to the scene of the crime.

Steven thought it was funny. "That ain't nothing. In the villages where I come from, if the men are away from the house, a baboon will just come on in with the woman standing there and take any food he sees right out of her kitchen. But if a man is there, he won't do it."

I never had the pleasure of talking with both Steven and Linus at the same time. But it was enjoyable speaking with them about each other. One morning as Linus was pointing out the names of various plants and shrubs, I asked him if it would be possible to go to a Masai village. He seemed flattered that I showed an interest in wanting to know more about his people. The visit had to be arranged with the tribal chief. I really wanted him to go along. He had a very good command of English along with the eagerness to spread the Masai gospel. But his work schedule at the hotel did not permit him to leave except on his day off.

"I will find you somebody to take you," he said. It was obvious that he was anxious for me to visit his tribe, although it wouldn't be the same without him.

As we walked along the trail, he showed me the

African green heart tree. The bark is used to make tea to ward off malaria. It seemed to me in talking with him that many people have this disease, but it can be controlled.

"Anytime that I begin to get that headache and fever coming on, the medicine man just fixes me a cup of tea and it goes away," he said.

I told him that there was quite a difference in the way that medicine was dispensed in America. "First, you have to get an appointment with a doctor, which is not easy. A prescription is written. This is taken to a pharmacist, the drug is given to you, and you are out more than $100. There is none of this boiling up some tree bark because it has to be approved by the Food and Drug Administration."

He looked at me in utter disbelief. "How could this be? I thought that everything was better in America."

"It's not better. It's just different."

His background and upbringing were totally different from mine. However, our conversation caused me to focus more on our similarities than our differences. As a man, he had the same bedrock needs, wants, and desires that I do. The love of his family, wanting the best for his children, having the basics of food, clothing, and shelter all seemed to dominate his life. In that respect, we were the same, except I prefer a little more solid nourishment than milk and blood.

"The four most important events in a man's life," he pontificated, "are his birth, circumcision, marriage, and death."

I found this to be a rather noteworthy comment because several times previously in conversation he had referred to the rites of circumcision as if it were some kind of celestial event. Having read my *National Geographic* articles and seen the *Nature* programs, I had some ideas about what takes place, but this was my opportunity of a lifetime to hear it firsthand from a real live tribesman.

"When a boy is about 14 or 15, he will mention to his father that he is ready to be circumcised. The father will always put him off and tell him that he is not ready. The boy then goes to other men in the tribe and tells them of his desire. He generally receives the same brush-off from them. It is necessary for him to persist until he finds someone who will take him seriously."

"What if a boy chooses not to be circumcised?"

"That could never happen."

"Why not?"

"Because a boy could never have sex with a woman until he has been circumcised."

"Never?"

"Never, never, never. That is tribal law."

"In America, circumcision is up to the parents, and the operation is performed in the hospital when the baby boy is born."

"You mean you would circumcise a baby?" he questioned in utter disbelief.

"What's wrong with that?"

"But how does a boy ever know when he becomes a man?" he asked curiously.

I had to think about that one. "I suppose when he gets his driver's license."

"You have some strange ways in America," he mused.

"I suppose you're right."

"My circumcision was the most important event in my whole life." He spoke with pride. "You see, a boy is never taken seriously and none of the elders ever pay much attention to him until after his circumcision. Then he becomes a man and can speak as a man with anyone. And it's the same with a woman."

"What about the women?" I asked with a bit of apprehension.

"They are circumcised just like the boys."

"How?"

"It's the same. When a girl reaches about the age of 14 or 15, the women of the tribe have a ceremony and her clitoris is cut out."

"What is the reason for doing this?"

"It is not proper for a woman to enjoy sex," he said matter-of-factly.

"What kind of ceremony is it?" I asked.

"I don't know." He shook his head.

"Why don't you know?"

"Because a man can never learn what goes on in the women's ceremony just like we never let them know what happens in the men's."

"Did you ever ask your wife?"

"No, I would never do that, and she would never ask me either. We are not supposed to know. I do know that the older women of the tribe counsel with the girls after their circumcision and tell them what they need to know the same way that we are told by the men of the tribe."

"Are you allowed to tell me what happened at your ceremony?"

"I suppose." He thought for a moment. "It is a very special thing. It has to be treated with reverence." He spoke with his eyes closed. "Once the elders have decided that a boy is ready, then the chief of the tribe confers with the chief of other neighboring Masai villages. The boys from the other villages are all brought together and the circumcisor arrives with his knife sharpened. Each one of us is brought before him with all of the adult males of our families standing around."

"What did you do? Were you scared?"

"We are not allowed to move a muscle or blink an eye. If I even slightly move a finger, it would bring so much shame and dishonor on me and my family that we would be forced to leave the village."

"That is amazing." I stood there in awe of this man as he revealed to me the secrets of his rights of passage into manhood.

"After the ceremony, there is a big celebration. The men make a beer out of the fruit of the sausage tree. I can tell you that is some strong stuff. All men and the new initiates go into a hut, and the beer sits in a large bowl in the middle of the floor. We have a plant that has a hollow stem like a straw. Some of them are 8, 10, and 12 feet long. Every man has a stem and sits around in a circle with one end of it in the bowl. That is the most fun. Everyone laughs and jokes and sings all night long. Then the boys are taken away to another place and stay with some older men who instruct them in what it is like to be a man. We stayed there from six months to a year before we were allowed to return to our villages."

"What did you do after you returned?" I asked.

"I went off to school."

"Do you have to pay for your schooling?"

"Yes, it costs a lot. My father had to pay 20 cows."

"I guess that is pretty expensive, isn't it?"

The Masais don't use money. It is of no use. Any money they receive is used to buy more cows. A man's wealth is determined by the number of cattle he owns. Linus' father also had to spend a lot of cows to buy his son a wife. Actually, it is a form of dowry which must be given to the father of the bride.

I asked him how he felt about his father choosing his wife for him.

"He only chooses my first wife," he answered. "Any other wives, I can choose for myself."

We stopped to admire a massive African green heart tree. Bark had been chipped away on various spots. Not only do they use it to ward off malaria, but also for women in childbirth.

Linus told me that when a baby is born, all men have to leave the village. The older women act as a midwife. They make a tea from the bark of this tree and mix it with animal fat. It takes away any soreness or pain. "That is some bad stuff to have to drink," he complained. "Man, it is bitter."

"Is there any kind of celebration for the newborn?"

"Oh, yes. All of the villagers stand around in a circle. The mother brings the baby out, and it is passed around for each person to hold and we all spit in its mouth."

"Spit in the baby's mouth?" I tried not to act too surprised.

"It gives the baby the immunities it needs to survive."

On the trip from Nairobi, we had seen a number of Masai villages and within a mile or so around the village you see young boys out tending the cattle or goats. Some of them appear to be no more than two or three years old. In fact, I was astounded to see some little kids who appeared as though they had just learned to walk out there in the wild all alone. I asked Linus about this.

"That's true," he said. "We send them out as early as possible to teach them about life. By the time a child starts to school, he will have three or four years' experience in managing a herd. The teachers say that they can always tell that a Masai child pays more attention than the others in school because they are not so easily detracted. They are more dependable and responsible. All children in our village have chores they must perform from the time they learn to walk."

"Yes, but isn't it dangerous for a little kid like that to be all alone? What about lions or hyenas?" I asked.

"Older men from the village will go out and check on them, but they never let the child know. It is necessary for the child to think that he is doing this duty alone."

"I notice that they always wear red. Is that to keep the animals away."

"That is Masai tradition," he responded proudly.

Linus was very interested to know what we thought of Africa and what we had been doing. He acted absolutely astounded that we had climbed to the top of Mount Kilimanjaro.

"How could you do that? I don't think it would be possible for me to go up that high. I am afraid of heights," he confessed.

"Listen, Linus, believe me that any man who can stand still and be circumcised without flinching can certainly climb Kilimanjaro."

He laughed.

The next day as we were having lunch, Linus came running in all excited.

"I have made arrangements for you to visit my village!"

"That's great! Can you go?"

"No, I have to work, but I have someone else who can take you."

I was disappointed but tried not to show it. I asked him if the person taking us was a Masai.

"No. He is a Luo. His name is Steven."

Steven drove slowly over the bumpy road covered with pot holes the size of the truck. Herds of zebras, wildebeest, gazelles, and antelopes roamed about. He had to stop so that a family of elephants could cross the road directly in front of the truck. They didn't pay any attention to us as if they could care less. We certainly didn't pose any threat to them. At one point, he steered the truck off the road into a bushy area. He seemed to instinctively know that a lioness had made a kill the night before and had brought the carcass there for her lazy husband and hungry cubs to devour. She always takes the leftovers, if any. The lion kingdom seems to be ripe for a good women's lib movement.

"Steven, do you ever see any snakes?" I asked knowing that Marie was absolutely petrified to even look at a picture of one.

"Not too many. The birds and mongooses eat a lot of them. But every once in a while, I'll drive up on a mamba."

"Isn't a mamba the most poisonous snake in the world?"

"I don't know, but I don't mess around with 'em. If I drive up next to one, I let my window up right away 'cause that snake will spit his poison right in your eye."

"You mean he can spit all the way from the ground up into the truck?" I was baiting him.

"You better believe he can, so you best keep your distance from 'em."

By this time, Marie was rolling up her window in a hurry.

"You're going to burn up," I told her.

"I don't care. I'd rather burn up than have a mamba spit in my eye."

I think that old Steven enjoyed embellishing a story, and he knew that he'd found a sucker with Marie in telling snake stories.

"You know, back in my village, anytime you go outside in the bush, you have to swing your arms way up in front of you and back of you, while you're walking 'cause you won't believe how fast a python can wrap around you. If he gets both your arms up against your body, then you are finished. All the time that he is wrapping you and squeezing the life out of you, he is licking you in the face with his old long fangs. The snake ain't poisonous but that stuff he licks on you makes your skin rot. But now if you got one of your arms free, you can fight that snake and get him off of you. Man, there have been plenty of times I've seen a python that had swallowed a goat or a calf. Not long ago, I saw one that swallowed a gazelle and his horns were still sticking out of that snake's mouth."

By that time, Marie had squirmed down into the foot of the truck. "Could we talk about something else?" she begged for mercy.

Steven loved it.

"How many children do you have, Steven?" she asked, attempting to change the subject.

"I've got me four girls," he responded.

"That must mean that you are going to get a lot of cows when your daughters get married," I kidded him.

But he seemed concerned that he did not have a son. "When the daughters get married, they move off to other tribal villages, but a son has to stay and look after his parents."

"Did you have to stay and look after your parents?" I asked.

"Well, you see, my father had seven wives, and in our tribe the first-born son of the first wife receives everything from the father when he dies. So it is his duty to take care of our father." Steven replied.

I asked him if he knew all of his brothers and sisters.

"Oh, yes, we all get together on occasions," he answered.

"Even all of the seven wives?"

"Yes, of course. Everyone gets along with each other."

I was curious why he had only one wife. "Why are you so different from your father?" I asked.

"Well, I've been thinking about getting me another one down here at Kichwa Tembo."

"Did your father choose your wife for you?"

"Yes, and I had to wrestle her to see if she was stronger."

"Wrestle her?"

"Yes, that is tradition in our tribe. Luos have big strong women. So you must wrestle her in front of the whole village. If she can pin you down, then you don't marry her."

"Well, I can certainly understand that. So I guess if you don't like the way she looks, then you can let her win. Is that right?"

"Yes, that's done, I'm sure." He laughed.

"You don't think you will ever have seven wives like your father?"

"No. My father is a rich man. He has hundreds of cows. He may be 85 years old but he still visits all seven of his wives, and he has never seen a doctor or the inside of a hospital."

"I believe it." I laughed.

About this time, the Masai village came into view. The chief was expecting us. He and his son greeted us, adorned in red plaid garments and fancy headdress, outside the fenced-in compound. The son of the chief had been educated at a boarding school and was the spokesman of the welcoming committee. He had studied African culture, Swahili, English, plant life, and animal husbandry. His use of English was very impressive. Being 21 and still unmarried was a bit unusual for a Masai. He had successfully convinced the old chief to hold off arranging his betrothal until he was ready. This was a modern concept that did not set too well with the chief.

After exchanging pleasantries and the necessary monetary gift, the gate to the village was opened, signaling their readiness to receive us. I looked around for Steven but the chief had instructed him to stay in the truck.

As we were escorted into the center of the ring of huts, the women's choir moved to a small hill nearby and serenaded us with songs and chants. I had a *déjà vu* flashback that I could be the great white hunter in a Tarzan movie surrounded by a sea of black faces. Fortunately, there were no boiling pots of water around, so my brief paranoia was quickly dispelled.

All the women had shaved heads and enough necklaces and beads to weigh down a good-sized rhinoceros. I would not call their ears "pierced," but "sliced" would be a better word. From the time they are babies, ear stretchers are used to make the holes larger. There was no way to count the number of ornaments hanging from their ears like Christmas trees. One woman had a brightly colored decoration the size of an oatmeal box that went through both of her ears and sat on the back of her neck. It caused me physical pain to look at it.

It seemed funny that the men obviously spent hours on their hairdos while the women had shaved heads. However, if a married woman is barren, or has not yet been circumcised, then she must let her hair grow. The men used red clay from the hills to color their hair in various shades of red and orange. Some had it plaited and braided in different designs and shapes, but all males certainly dedicated a considerable amount of time to hairdressing.

Both men and women were always attired in some shade of red. The women wore no shoes, but the men had sandals. Being tall people, it seemed strange to me that their huts, which lined the perimeter of the village, were no more than chest high. Constructed of sticks, branches, and straw, then covered with cow dung, the huts apparently did not leak. The three rooms were used for sleeping by the family members as well as the newborn calves and goats. Since their diet consists only of milk and blood, they need no kitchen for cooking. It was a cozy arrangement to say the least.

David was the name of the chief's son and served as our escort around the tribal village.

"What religious beliefs do the people have here?" I asked, knowing that the day was Sunday.

"All Masais are Christian," he answered emphatically.

"Do you hold worship services?"

"Sometimes we do. It depends on whatever the chief wants to do."

"But as Christians, you allow a man to have many wives, don't you?" It seemed inconsistent to me.

"Of course, that is Masai tradition." He shrugged, obviously finding no inconsistency in that.

I also questioned him about Steven's accusation that Masais have continued to practice the art of cattle stealing. It caught me by surprise that David readily admitted it and saw nothing wrong with it. "Masai tradition" justifies almost everything, I suppose.

In lawyerly fashion, I attempted to cross-examine him about how the tribe metes out justice among its inhabitants.

"The chief and elder men of the tribe make the decision about any conflicts."

"What happens if they find that someone has done something wrong or has violated some tribal law?"

"Then his best bull is slaughtered."

"Is that all?"

"Yes."

"You don't tie him to a post and whip him?"

He laughed at my ridiculous remark.

After attempting to sell us all kinds of beads, earrings, and trinkets, we were then treated to a dance of the warriors. The men sang, but it was more like shouts and screams than singing. During their performance, each one took turns jumping as high as he could while standing in one place. It was amazing how high some of them could jump. They put Michael Jordan to shame.

Linus had warned me that some of the little children might try to run up and touch my skin because they had never seen a white man, especially with hair on his arms. I did get some strange and inquiring looks, but no one tried to touch me.

Although we would love to have stayed there much longer, we were scheduled to fly back to Nairobi. The people waved their goodbyes to the pale-skinned American couple.

Our ways of living are much different from theirs, but not necessarily better. If there was any stress, tension, or unhappiness in that village totally devoid of modern technology, they certainly kept it well concealed. Their pleasant smiles and bright eyes told a story of contentment. It seemed pretty obvious to me that they had no desire or intention of changing their way of life. The "Masai traditions" appeared to be inviolate. While David was a young, educated man, his ambition and plan was to someday be like his father. He would never own a car or a stereo, or a television, and he could care less. That Great Rift Valley in Western Kenya would be his home forever, and I suspect his children and grandchildren as well.

Steven waited patiently in the truck.

"I thought you would go in with us?" I asked him.

"That chief would not allow a Luo in his village. I guess he thought I might steal one of their cows," he laughed.

As the old DC-3 was about to land, it was Steven's duty to drive his truck down the runway in front of the plane to clear off the zebras, wildebeest, and a couple of ostriches. They scampered away when Steven "sat down" on his horn.

A few passengers got off the DC-3 to relieve themselves out in the open behind the plane. The pilot doubled as baggage boy. Since there was no flight attendant, he yelled to the passengers, "There's a cooler back there in the rear of the plane if anybody wants anything to drink."

I couldn't help but laugh as I compared this to our orderly and efficient manner of flight service back home.

As we taxied down the runway, I saw that big old Luo, Steven, a character from the word go. Linus arrived after we boarded the plane and drove up in a truck beside Steven. We regretted not having had a chance to tell him of our visit to his village or to thank him for being our friend. It seemed to be left in the hands of Steven to convey that message to him. What would be said by him, an avowed enemy of the Masai? We will never know.

The plane gained altitude and the two of them became smaller and smaller. My thoughts were that their ancestors could not have talked with each other and their encounters would have been only with spears. Though there was still a chasm separating Steven and Linus, at least they were talking. Perhaps their children would do even better.

THE RUFUS LETTER

CHAPTER EIGHT

CHAPTER 8

THE RUFUS LETTER

Rufus, Tom's loyal and trusted golden retriever, had been lodged in the County Jail for dogs on five occasions because of digging under a neighbor's fence to visit her female dog in heat. The irate owner hired a lawyer to sue for damages. Here is Tom's response to the lawyer's demand.

February 22, 1984

Robert D. Miles, Esq.,
Attorney at Law
P.O. Box 1022
Brunswick, Georgia 31521

Dear Mr. Miles:

I received your letter of February 6, 1984, regarding my dog's escapades with those of your client's. Now Rufus is a very nice and personable Golden Retriever who lives with Marie, my two sons, and me. His affection has made him a friend of everyone on the beach, even the tourists who are here for only one week in the summer. Though he is a beautiful dog who jogs with me on the beach and knows no stranger, he is not perfect. Like many of us males, he seems to have an incurable case of horniness. Even though I am aware of this hideous fault, I can't help but feel a certain amount of empathy for him and his malady.

I have talked with him about the probability that his lewd and licentious behavior may subject him to legal action and he could lose all of his worldly possessions. I have even scolded him repeatedly to stay away from bitches in heat, but he always smiles and looks at me with a twinkle in his eye as if to say that, as a self-avowed hypocrite, I don't always practice what I preach.

I do not in any way wish to minimize the dastardly complaints of your client, for nothing is more bothersome than someone else's trespassing dog. So I have not sat idly by and allowed this to continue. I conferred with Billy Weeks, D.V.M., about removing the poor devil's testicles, a subject that makes any male flinch to even speak of it. But I am told that because the pattern has been set and that even though he may be physically unable to perform the act, he will continue to believe that he can. He will still sniff around the females with all pretense of being a valid paramour, which is not unlike a lot of older lawyers that I have observed bragging about their improbable conquests.

Since no type of operation on his privates will be to any avail, we have confined him permanently to our front deck and have admonished him to think high and lofty thoughts. And, if the temptation to live his old life as a gigolo becomes so great that it becomes physically obvious, then I will take him for a swim in the cold sea water to douse his passion.

Even though Rufus will never be truly satisfied again, I do hope that your client will find my actions to be sincere and satisfactory to her. I feel certain that the declining years of his life will not be for naught. He has had some right enviable experiences that will make for some rather nice memories on those spring nights when the moon is full and the flowers are in bloom. I have heard it said and believe it with all of my heart that young men see visions and old men dream dreams, and sometimes fantasy is much better than the real thing.

Sincerely,

Thomas E. Dennard, Jr.

TED/pcn
c.c. Rufus

A LETTER TO SUSAN TO SHARE WITH HER SONS

CHAPTER 9

A LETTER TO SUSAN TO SHARE WITH HER SONS

My dear, sweet daughter,

It's such a cliché to say that "time flies" and "kids grow up so fast," but how true it is. It somehow defies even the imagination to think that you are now old enough to be married and have kids of your own. I don't think it would surprise me a bit if one morning you woke us by jumping up and down on our bed. It seems like such a short time ago when that was a daily happening. Memories are wonderful treasures to call upon when we are in the mood to reminisce, and there's nothing wrong with thinking of the good times and smiling. But life must go on, and it's not good to cling to the past.

I've been around for a few years and traveled to a lot of different places in the world. I've seen so many things, met countless new faces of various cultures, and have a storehouse full of experiences. I'm extremely fortunate to gain this knowledge of foreign countries and people, but the main thing that all of my travels and adventures have taught me most is about myself.

I think you know me well enough by now that I

don't need to outline my philosophy of life to you. But if I could somehow talk to your baby boys on a man-to-man basis to teach them some of the things that I have had to learn the hard way, this is what I would like for them to know about me.

1. First and foremost, **WE SHOULD NOT TAKE OURSELVES TOO SERIOUSLY**.

This is by far the biggest fault that I see in most people, and I certainly have a large dose of this malady myself.

I run into lawyers, doctors, preachers, bankers, educators, bureaucrats, writers, and others who appear to have an inflated idea of their self-worth. It seems to come about from our failure to put things in proper perspective. We have become experts in making mountains out of mole hills.

When I was in the Himalayas, there were more stars and bright objects in the sky than I had ever seen in my life. It was mind-blowing to be literally on "the top of the world" standing on the highest mountains of this planet. What it does is to help put things in proper perspective. We are such an infinitesimal part of the whole network, no more than a breath of air or a blink of the eye. If a human body could somehow represent the whole of creation, then we would be like one tiny cell on that body.

You know those rocks I keep on my desk. Some are from the tops of mountains I have climbed; there's a large one from the Berlin Wall and others from around the globe. But one in particular is from an island in the North Sea that is estimated to be over a billion years old. When I get frustrated from the day's happenings, or more likely, if I am feeling my importance, then I take a look at that rock. It's been around about 20 million times as many years as I have lived and will probably be here about that same amount of time after I'm gone.

Sometimes we think the whole universe revolves around us and that we will be sorely missed when we're gone. Believe me, the world will not skip a beat. It keeps right on chugging along. So, we should "lighten up," "chill out," "sit loose in the saddle," and "enjoy life." These thoughts bring about the second point.

2. HAVE A SENSE OF HUMOR.

It is essential to laugh a lot, and some of that needs to be directed toward ourselves. Our good health depends upon it. Stress, worry, and anxiety bring about a world of problems for the mind and body to have to deal with. If we allow those things to continue to exist in our life, then we will eventually have some kind of physical ailment as a result of it. We all need to work more on bringing joy into our lives. You may say, how can I be joyful when there is so much sadness going on in the world? And that's when it becomes important to resign ourselves to divine order, which brings about the third point.

3. FAITH

I have wrestled with religion all of my life. You know, when I was growing up, my mama made me to go church every time the doors were opened. When I left home and went to Davidson College, I was required to study Bible, one year of the Old Testament and one year of the New Testament. So my formative years were immersed in the fundamentals of the

Christian faith. Later, I became enamored with Eastern religions and even stayed some time in an Indian ashram and in a Buddhist monastery. The greater part of my life has been spent in searching and probing through religious doctrines for answers to find truth. I have had some profound spiritual experiences like the one at Mount Everest. But one day it dawned on me that my main problem was in making the whole thing too complicated.

Let's face it, life and death are complex subjects, but there is no point in beating our brains out over something that we can never know for sure during this lifetime. As I see it, there is only one key to it, and that is accepting, in childlike faith, that a Supreme Being exists. There is a religious sect in India that has no name for God because the mere fact of a name is somehow limiting to Its divine nature. It doesn't matter so much what we call this Being, so long as we affirm that It exists and then live constantly with that knowledge. We should learn to keep it in the back of our minds all the time.

Jesus said it best when he said that all the commandments can be summed up in only two: just love God and love and respect your fellow beings. In order to do this, it requires surrender, throwing up the white flag to all of our headstrong ways, and accepting these eternal and ultimate truths.

One might say that this is a cop-out. Why should we hand over our problems to a Supreme Being rather than dealing with them ourselves? I find that if I dwell on the dark sides of life, then I start getting mired down in a boghole. Some problems just can't be resolved by me or any other human being. While it's not good to just sweep them under the rug, it works for me to believe that I can turn them over to a higher power.

A LETTER TO SUSAN

Now getting back to the first two points, it is not necessary to take ourselves very seriously once we have made this surrender pact with the Almighty. And it can be joyful and happy once we have shifted that burden. In fact, I believe that it is sacrilegious to worry. Remember the admonition, don't be anxious about tomorrow, let tomorrow be anxious for itself. If troubles and sorrows are dished out to us, then we need to give 100 percent effort to do what should be done to rid ourselves of the problem, but once we have done the best we can, then we have to surrender the rest to the Almighty and trust that it will be justly taken care of.

There is another point we must know that is essential about religion. It is not sufficient just to know the eternal truths; we must put them into practice. So we must live our lives in that manner. To keep myself in line and attempt to practice what I preach, it is necessary to at least daily commune with the spirit. I run out of gas if I don't refuel everyday. My life is somewhat like listening to a radio where in time the station begins to get a little fuzzy. I have to take the dial and fine tune it back onto the station so it will come in loud and clear. This can be done in daily reading words of inspiration, praying, and/or meditating. Some people may get by with just one of those, but for me, it's best to do all three. The everyday problems then become tolerable because I can more easily put them in proper perspective.

Believe me, I cannot stress enough the importance of finding this faith. It is not necessary to jump through all of the hoops that I did. The way is probably different for each person. But if one has not yet found it, then it's necessary to keep searching and seeking and it can be found.

wis said, "If I believe, have faith, live a
d get to the end of my way and find that
10ax, then what have I lost? But if I have
no ιαια., n't believe, and get to the end and find
that it was true, then I have lost it all."

4. TRY OUR BEST TO FIND OUT WHO WE ARE AND THEN DELIGHT IN BEING THAT PERSON.

Too often we compare ourselves with other
people and are much too concerned with what others might think of our actions. Remember that our
pact is with God, not with anyone else. That is not to
say that we can't improve ourselves or be better
persons. But, believe me, if we truly feel that who we
are and what we do would please the Almighty and
also ourselves, then we don't need to care about
what other people are going to say about us.

Don't ever waste time trying to conform to society. Can you think of one great person in all of history
who was a conformist to society's dictates. One who
strives to be like others sometimes has a tendency to
think and say the worst. They feel that if they belittle
another person, then it somehow elevates them above
that person. We truly arrive at the pinnacle when it is
realized that we are equal with all people.

It is absolutely necessary to "know thyself" and
once we do, then we should strive to be that person.
It's okay to be different. It's not necessary to be like
everybody else. God sets pretty high standards, and
I also set my own standards. So I feel that if I can
meet this test, then that's all that matters.

I have a friend who tells me that he can't know
himself because he is more than one person. Being a
Gemini, I have a good understanding about having

more than one personality. But I say we need to get in touch with all aspects of our being and attempt to know as much as we can about ourselves no matter how complex we may be.

I believe that we should liken the world to a big flower bush with every flower on it being distinct. God sees us all as flowers, but we seem to concern ourselves too much with the difference in all of the flowers. Let's pretend that you are a rose and I am a daisy and someone else is a lily and so on. No matter how much I may try, I can't be a rose or a lily. I have to be a daisy. So I need to put into practice being the prettiest and best daisy that I can be. If God had wanted me to be a rose or a lily, then He would have made me one.

Some people are so worried about the kinds of flower that they are. They are afraid to show any parts of themselves that are different from others or might cause them to be criticized. So, as a result, their flowers don't bloom. Have you ever seen roses where the buds never open? They just wither and die as buds and never blossom. It is sad, but there are a lot of people like that. A person may not like the kind of flower he or she is, but we should do our best to make our flowers bloom and be as pretty as we know how to be.

I remember my experiences in the early 1970s when I backpacked around Eastern Europe and North Africa with my long hair, jeans, T-shirt, sandals, and sunglasses. In countries like Bulgaria, Romania, Hungary, Poland, and Morocco, I was a complete oddity. Most people had never seen anyone like me. In some places, I was treated pretty badly because of being an American and having long hair.

My appearance represented freedom to be who I

wanted to be and that was something they didn't have. I was pushed out of a taxi in Sofia onto the street because of the way I looked. I was removed from a train car headed toward the Black Sea and placed in isolation because my appearance was causing too much of a disturbance. I was forced to leave East Germany the night of arrival, escorted by guards armed with submachine guns and literally shoved off the train. I was informed on a bus to Marrakesh that I would be killed in the next town because my hair was too long.

All of which is to say that I have seen hatred in people's eyes when they looked at me merely because I had a different appearance from them. Now, as I look back on it, I wouldn't change a thing. I knew that I had no ill will toward anyone, and it was okay for me to be the person who I felt was me. It was those moments that gave me some inkling of what it might have been like to be black in a white society. Those experiences have helped me to be more tolerant and understanding of minorities and the underprivileged.

So I would tell my grandsons, "Be who you are, no more, no less. Tread lightly upon this Earth. Don't harm another, and allow others to be who they are without judging them."

5. BE THANKFUL AND APPRECIATIVE AT ALL TIMES.

As often as possible, give thanks to God. Life is a very special gift, and we should never take it for granted. Every time there is a spare moment during the day or night, say, "Thank you." It will then become a habit that will make us more appreciative of the good things that we have in our lives.

A Buddhist would say that we must also be thankful for the bad things in our lives as well. They would contend that the problems of life are necessary ingredients to make us strong, so we must thank God when He gives us an obstacle to cross over. The theory of this is that any old tugboat can sail on smooth waters, but to test the true strength of a vessel, we must see how it handles on stormy seas. If it can pass through the turbulence without sinking, then we know it is seaworthy.

There is an old Taoist parable (repeated in *The Te Of Piglet* by Benjamin Hoff) where a farmer and his son live alone out in the countryside. A neighbor comes over to console the farmer whose only horse had run away.

"Oh, that's bad!" the neighbor said.

"Maybe not," replied the farmer.

In time the horse returned with several wild horses that had joined him.

"Oh, that's good!" the neighbor rejoiced.

"Maybe not," replied the farmer.

Shortly afterwards, the son's leg was broken when he was thrown from one of the wild horses.

"Oh, that's bad!" the neighbor said, attempting to convey sympathy.

"Maybe not," replied the farmer.

Soon the army came looking for youths to go to war, but couldn't take the son because of his broken leg. And so on, and so, and so on.

There is a lesson to be learned from this. We all have a tendency to want to label events in our lives as being bad or good because that's how we perceive them at the time. But bad can blend into good and good can blend into bad. We need to alter our perception of life's happenings as being good or bad and realize that every occurrence is necessary to make us who we are.

Saint Paul said that we should rejoice in our sufferings, knowing that suffering produces endurance, and endurance produces character, and character produces hope, and hope will never disappoint us. So we must be thankful and appreciative all of the time for the good and bad in our lives. This will cause us to have a good disposition and attitude toward the happenings in our lives and help us to better deal with our fellow beings. By making this a habit, we are then able to meet life everyday with as much enthusiasm as we can muster, and it will keep the drudgeries from getting us down.

6. **LIFE IS SHORT.**

The Buddhists say that life is as fleeting as a house on fire. When we are young, time seems to last forever, and the older we get, the faster time flies. I have heard older people say that all of my life, and I never paid much attention to it. Now I know that it is true. It amazes me how quickly Christmas comes around each year. Although I still feel young, there are people younger than I am dying all the time.

Now, on the other hand, we shouldn't get bogged down and stressed out worrying over how short life is. That would be like someone who can't enjoy a roller coaster ride because the mind keeps telling them that soon it will be over.

I like to think of life as an extended vacation in France. While I am there, I want to make the most of it. I want to enjoy myself and have a good time, so that when I do go home, I can feel that it was all worthwhile. While I am on a vacation, I have the inner feeling that the time is going to be short, so I want to get everything out of it that I can. That's also the way I feel about my life. I don't know when I'm going to have to board the plane and fly home, so I want to live life to the fullest. Auntie Mame said, "Life is a banquet and most poor fools are starving to death." Believe me, I like to eat and I want to participate in the banquet.

In order to do that, we must get our priorities straight. It is necessary to work to make a living, but we should always select a work that we enjoy doing. If we like it, then it's not work. In America we seem to only look at how much money can be made. I have learned that money should definitely not be the criteria for choosing a job. If we can make enough to have the basic necessities of life, then that's what really matters. I believe we should do our best in our work, but save some time to play.

Some people get so wrapped up in their work that it's the only thing they can think about. I say, don't over do it. I have never heard a dying man say that he wished he had spent more time at the office. Most people at the end of their road regret not having taken more time to play or spend time with their families and friends or doing the things that they enjoy doing best.

While our work may be very important, the chances are that it is not nearly as important as we think it is. I advocate giving it 100 percent while working and do the very best job that can be done. It will be much more fulfilling if I do. It is said that we get out of something what we put into it. I believe that is true. But then we should walk away from it and not take it home with us. Finding a hobby that is fun and relaxing will enrich our lives. Then we should spend a lot of quality time with our avocation as well as our vocation. I have my hostel and traveling to keep me excited and give me something to look forward to. For each person, it is different, but we all need to find whatever it is in life that is fun to do and do it!

7. DON'T SPREAD OURSELVES TOO THIN

One of the biggest problems that I must try to overcome and need to learn most about is the old saying of "DON'T SPREAD OURSELVES TOO THIN." There is so much in life that excites me that I find myself not giving quality time to any of it. The other thing that I have had to learn from a whole lot of experience is to learn to say NO. In the past, anytime anyone asked me to do something, I always felt some moral obligation to do it. As a result, I was in every organization that one can imagine and was president of many of them.

It is okay to join things, but we should pick and choose what we want to belong to and not let others do it for us. Only become a member of an organization that creates within a feeling of zeal and passion and promotes worthwhile causes. Personally, I have narrowed my long list of memberships to environmental organizations because that's one subject I feel most strongly about. If we have too many irons in the fire, we always wind up chasing our tails. Then we don't have much satisfaction from any of them. We shouldn't be a member of any group unless we are going to dedicate some quality time to it. Again, we get out of something what we put into it. So, I would tell my grandsons, "Be selective in what you undertake, and then give it your best."

8. **WORK ON KEEPING OUR WHOLE BEING IN GOOD SHAPE.**

For as long as you have known me, I have tried to keep my physical body in good condition. From the time you were a baby, I played basketball and jogged until my knees finally gave out. Even today, I still work out at the gym, ride bikes, hike, and canoe. For two different periods of my life, I was a vegetarian and have always tried to pay attention to eating healthy food. I am convinced that it is essential to keep the temple that houses the soul in as good a shape as possible.

But after all of those years of working out, I learned that it is not sufficient just to concentrate on the body. It is absolutely necessary to keep the mind and the soul in tiptop shape as well. So many athletes I have known over the years are frequently sick or stressed out in some kind of way. Too often they become obsessed with their physical bodies and lose sight of the mental tension they have created for themselves. I strongly advocate some kind of physical exercise, but it is extremely important to keep it in proper perspective. It is just as important to spend some time resting and relaxing and doing nothing.

The brain is a muscle that requires exercising just as much as the rest of the physical body. How many times have I seen mentally active people retire. When I meet them a couple of years later, they act like they have Alzheimer's disease. It is hard to believe that this is the same person I once knew. The mind gets dull if it is not exercised and challenged. If we are not required to retire, then we probably shouldn't do it. But if we have to quit work, then we should take up some hobby that keeps the mind alert and strong.

As I have said before, the spirit has to be active inside the body. "The kingdom of heaven is within," according to the Bible. We can't just leave it dormant while waiting to shed our physical shells. It is necessary to get in touch with the spirit and develop a good line of communication with it. For each person, the manner of doing this may be different, but for me, it is through meditation.

My mind must become devoid of any thoughts, and then I can listen to what the spirit has to say. I can tell you that I have had some very profound and enlightening moments in my meditations. But even if nothing earthshaking comes from it, I am accomplishing the greatest form of mental and physical relaxation that I know anything about. It takes away tension, stress, and pressure, and permits me to be at ease. Daily activities have a tendency to get my wires all crossed up. Meditation is very important in helping to maintain some kind of balance and allows me to get the dial tuned in to a clear channel.

9. **MODERATION**

This should be the key word in everything we do. Don't eat too much, drink too much, work too much, play too much, work out too much, and so on and so on. I don't think it's necessary to be a teetotaler with anything unless it is too detrimental to my health. Just intake, consume, and live our whole lives in moderation.

To say, as I have said in the past, "I don't eat any meat," or as some people say, "I would definitely not allow alcohol to touch my lips," all has a tendency to make us tense, uptight, and self-righteous. While I don't really care for the taste of meat, if I go to someone's home where it is served, I just take a small quantity and, so far, it hasn't killed me yet. Believe me, I have eaten some strange and exotic things in my travels around the world. Some of it has been hard to swallow, but I do my best to relax and just take what comes along. Fortunately, I have been blessed with a strong stomach.

10. AM I FUN TO BE WITH?

We should seriously take a look at ourselves and ask this poignant question, "Am I fun to be with?" Think about it. When our friends are around, are we so serious and calculating about everything we do and say that it makes everyone feel ill at ease? Have you ever been around people who act like Chicken Little? The sky is always falling. Those kinds of people are depressing. They take all the fun out of life. This goes back to the first two things I mentioned in this epistle. Don't take ourselves too seriously and have a sense of humor.

When we greet our spouses each night, are our dispositions such that it should make them glad to see us? Shouldn't we take a hard look at ourselves to see whether or not we are fun to be around?

Over the years, I have counseled hundreds of marriages. I am told how dreadfully they are treated by their spouses, and how they are not appreciated at all. The one thing I learned in the beginning about listening to domestic problems is that always there are two sides to the story. I haven't heard it all if I have just listened to one of them. As I sit there, observing the tension, stress, and tightness in their bodies, I always wonder what they have contributed to the horrible conditions in their lives.

Very often, at a most opportune time, I will pop the question, "Are you fun to be with?" This is always a show-stopper. They look at me in utter disbelief, like what in the world has that got to do with anything? I tell them it has a lot to do with everything in our lives. Who wants to go home every night to a bore? I ask them if they meet their husbands or wives by telling them all of the troubles of the day? Is it possible to just lighten up a little bit and try to have a little fun with marriage? Let's think. When was the last time we took a walk on the beach with our spouses in the moonlight? When was the last time that just the two of us ate by candlelight with only music in the background? When was the last time that just the two of us went on a picnic? When was the last time that the two of us sat alone in silence and just talked? Most of my clients answer all of these questions with a resounding, "NEVER."

It takes a little effort to do those things, but it will pay off big dividends in the long run. Because, who knows, it may cause us to wind up being happy, something that many couples can't fathom. I tell my clients that there is no one in the world standing between us and happiness except ourselves. The prison in which we find ourselves is surrounded by the walls that we have constructed. In fact, most of the unhappiness created within us is then transposed to our spouses. It's so easy to blame our spouses for all of our problems. Generally, we use them as a scapegoat. Now don't get me wrong, I don't badger all of my clients by making them feel like they are the only guilty party. At least half the time, they are not. But I want to make sure that they have tried everything they can to save the marriage.

A fault that I find with most marriages is that

one, or maybe both of them, expects too much out of the other. One thing that I have learned about human beings over the years is that we should not expect too much out of them. I would rather be pleasantly surprised by their kindness than to expect it and not get it. And that is doubly true between spouses. After all, we are just human. If we can find a mate who has seven or eight good points and two or three bad points, we should consider ourselves lucky. But what that means is that we have to learn to live with those two or three bad points.

It's like playing cards. When the hands are dealt out, we are not going to get all face cards every time. We have to learn to play the hand we're dealt. And that is extremely true with a marriage. Don't sit around moaning about not having the ace of spades or the king of diamonds. But look at the good cards you have been dealt and play them to the fullest.

Don't always be thinking that the grass is going to be greener on the other side of the fence. Generally, we are sadly disappointed to find out that it is not. It's like the drinking glass that is filled halfway to the top. Some people look at it as being half filled and others look at it as being half empty. If we see roses blooming, surrounded by garbage, can we not enjoy the roses?

I like the scene in the movie, *Fried Green Tomatoes*, when Kathy Bates wrapped herself in cellophane to meet her husband at the door. Why not? It's good to put a little spice in one's life. Do something different for a change. Don't just live in the same old rut day after day after day. If our spouses are taking everything too seriously, then we need to help them out of the drudgery and routine, which will add a little zest to both of our lives.

I am often asked, usually by a close relative, "When are you going to grow up?" My answer is normally, "I hope never." There is no way to subtract the years from one's age, but we can always be young at heart. I still like to do fun things. If that is immature, then I plead guilty. "When are you going to stop building tree houses?" I probably never will. No one has ever been able to convince me of the value of acting old. It is so refreshing for me to meet someone in their 70's, 80's, or even 90's, who is still high on life. I have met a few of them hiking on mountain trails in various parts of the world. It reassures me that maybe I can be like them when I grow up.

But whether we are young, old, or middle-aged, we should at least once a day, ask ourselves the question, "Am I fun to be with?" If we can keep it in the back of our minds, it will do wonders for us and everyone else around us.

11. **MONEY**

This has been a hard one for me. Being a product of parents of the depression, too much emphasis in my youth was placed on having money and then saving as much as humanly possible. No one ever told me that the first consideration in determining employment should be based on my love for the work. For me, it was all a matter of numbers. How much does it pay? There was an awful lot of unlearning that needed to take place in my life.

I had blindly followed this materialistic practice until a very profound experience hit me. My travels in foreign countries introduced me to people, who by all appearances were much happier than the ones I knew back home, and they had virtually no money or things. It caused me to do a lot of rethinking.

I have been extremely lucky and have most of my life lived in a beach house on the Atlantic Ocean with spectacular views of the sunrises and sunsets. While I certainly haven't accumulated much money, I do have property in the forest where the Hostel is located, and the value of these two properties is considerable. So it's pretty hypocritical of me to talk about the advantages of having bare necessities.

But I think it all has to do with where we place our priorities. Can I live happily without these things? Yes, I believe I can. Do I want more? No, I don't. Some Americans have received their black belt in greed. The more they have, the more they want. Their value system is based on what they possess and they somehow feel that this elevates them above those who don't have as much. Like playing monopoly, the one who has the most money at the end of the game wins.

It has been my observation, that the more money and things that a person has, the more problems are created. I'm not, by any means, saying that the poorer we are, the happier we will be. But we should all pay more attention to only possessing what is really needed without all the excess baggage. Perhaps it is necessary to accumulate a lot of money and things in order to realize how meaningless they all are.

One thing that bothers me most about a lot of Americans is that we have become so soft. We have feathered our nest with so many gadgets and material things to the extent that I'm afraid that many of us couldn't live without them. I admit that I have about ten times more of these things than I really need that I seem to use daily. But why is it that I feel so at home when I'm out in the wilderness sleeping next to a stream or a waterfall. I don't miss those things at all, and furthermore, it makes me feel good about myself that I can actually live very well without them.

I'm afraid that if some foreign power or aliens from another planet took all of our property and material things away from us and threw us out to survive on our own, a lot of people wouldn't have any idea how to manage. I think that's bad. Maybe we should require every American to take one week a year and go on an Outward Bound survival trip to learn that we can exist very well without all our conveniences.

Recently, a woman swelled with pride as she told me how well her son was doing. "He's an engineer making $60,000 a year." I looked at her, waiting to hear the rest of her story, but that was it. From that one statement, am I to assume that he is doing well? I wanted to say, "Is he happy? Does he love his work? Does he have peace of mind?" But to her, that was sufficient to prove that he was a success.

Jesus said that it is easier for a camel to go through the eye of a needle than a rich man to enter the kingdom of heaven. There are a lot of people in this country who claim to be Christians, but this philosophy is somewhat contradictory to our capitalistic values. We are taught the theory that more is better. If Jesus is right that having a lot of money makes it more difficult to get into heaven, then why are so many Christians trying their best to make more and more money?

It's not that money and materialism are necessarily bad things, in and of themselves, but it is the love of money and the attachment to material things that causes us to go astray. There are many good books on the subject of living a more simple life, but one that I especially like is *Small Is Beautiful*. Read it sometime.

I have seen a lot of businessmen who allow money to be the sole factor in making all of their decisions. There was a period in my life when I went along with that idea. I think it was hard for me to see the full perspective because I was standing right on top of it. When I was far away in some foreign country, it became easier for me to place these values in some kind of order. I could get out of my rut and look down at my life and try to determine if I was satisfied with the progress of it.

They say that age is a state of mind. Well, so is happiness. Although it is completely antagonistic to our economic system, I am convinced that it is best to strive to live a more simple life. We should set aside some time to do the things we like to do. While I'm not opposed to work, I meet a lot of people who are obsessed with it. Some men use their wives and children as an excuse for having to work so hard. It is completely contradictory because probably what the wife and children need more than the money is to have him around the house being a husband and father.

Television, radio, newspapers, and magazines are constantly bombarding us with advertisements trying to persuade us to buy something. They strive to convince us that we need to purchase a particular item to make us happy or to be with the "in crowd." Why don't we restrain ourselves from falling for these gimmicks? Why buy what we don't really need?

We Americans spend billions on cosmetics to beautify ourselves. It seems that the more we try to make the surface of our bodies more beautiful, the uglier we become internally. If we would strive to improve ourselves from the inside, then it would work magic with the exterior. The best thing we can put on our faces to become more attractive is a smile.

I have been told that the richest person in the world is the one who has a lot of things that money can't buy, such as love in the heart for God and our fellow beings, peace of mind, happiness, heartfelt joy, good health, true friends, loving family relations, an eye for beauty, a good sense of humor, the desire to help others, and the knowledge that God is the source of all good. These are the things that we need to strive for, the nonmaterial values of life. We seem to think that having a lot of money will permit us to have all of this, but it doesn't. Happiness is often found in watching a sunrise or a sunset or seeing the twinkle in a baby's eye or being in the midst of nature and none of that costs a thing.

You know, I have done a great deal in helping other people plan their estates. It really baffles me to see people who want to amass large sums of money and property to pass on to their children. So many times after the parents die, I have seen the children fight over what they feel they are entitled to receive and then blow it all once they get it. I believe that we only appreciate what we have personally worked for and made on our own.

The only things that parents should give their kids is a good philosophy of life, a proper value system, a good education, and the tools to make it on their own. Teach them independence and how to stand on their own two feet without being dependent on us. These are the things that they will appreciate most.

We definitely cannot take it with us, so we should concentrate on living life in moderation. Don't get too caught up in having a lot of money and material things. Jesus said it best when He told us not to store up for ourselves treasures on earth for thieves to steal and rust to corrupt, but to store up for ourselves treasures in heaven, those spiritual things that no one can take away from us.

12. **FORGIVENESS**

This is one of the real cornerstones if we ever want to find true happiness. To forgive can be a difficult thing to do. When someone has said something ugly about us or has harmed us in some kind of way, at first we feel hurt, then anger, and then perhaps revenge. If we carry the hurt and anger around with us, it is like a cancer that eats on us with slow painful bites. As hard as it may be, we would be doing ourselves a big favor if we could just forgive the person. Release will come to our spirits and that hurtful cancer will then go away.

Anytime I tell someone this, they always say, "But do you know what so and so did to me?" And they will repeat it again in order to emphasize how they are justified in feeling the way that they do. I can tell you that I have heard some pretty horrible things in the law office. It is unbelievable to me the number of women who have experienced the horror of being sexually abused as a child by a father, uncle, or some other adult male. And it's not just women who have been sexually abused. A lot of men have had the same experience. There are multitudes of adults who carry emotional scars and hurts from childhood, and many of them have had extremely sad lives.

Sometimes I feel angry when I hear what clients are telling me. But in my heart I am absolutely convinced that the only way to heal these hurts is to forgive the person who committed the wrong. As hard as that may be to do, it is essential for our good health.

An equally important ingredient in the healing process is to forgive ourselves. Not only have bad things been inflicted upon us by others, but we have also committed our share of wrongs, too. There is absolutely no way under the sun to undo the past. It has come and gone. We can only deal with our present and whatever future lies ahead. So we also need forgiveness from ourselves. It is detrimental to our well-being to go around feeling guilty. We have to shed ourselves of whatever guilt that others have inflicted upon us as well as what we have inflicted upon ourselves.

It is said that we hurt others because either we have been hurt or because we expect to be hurt.

The Bible says that to err is human, to forgive is divine.

Laurence Sterne said, "Only the brave know how to forgive. A coward never forgave; it is not in his nature."

One of Jesus' final acts upon the cross was to forgive those who were crucifying him. "Father, forgive them for they know not what they do."

As the Lord has forgiven you, so you also must forgive. Colossians 3:13.

13. **PATIENCE**

Now this is another hard one for me and probably a lot of other people. I'm afraid that genetically I was cheated in not getting my fair share. Both my father and grandfather had a real shortage of patience. As for me, I like for things to occur in a timely fashion, which, of course, they do. But I want it on my schedule rather than having to wait around on divine order. Although, I'm much better about it now than I used to be, there is still plenty of room for improvement.

It is said that impatience is a lack of confidence in God. If we will completely surrender to God's will, then we just let go, and let God's way prevail. This does not mean that we shouldn't give 100 percent effort on everything we undertake. But the progress of it and the results of it should be left in the hands of God. There is no point in feeling that we need to move from one point to another as fast as possible. Let's take our time, pass slowly along our trail, and learn the lessons that are put there before us.

Remember, behind every dark cloud and difficulty, there is a hidden blessing. Things don't always work out as we plan them, but we must not forget that God's way is the right way. Remember the saying that all things work together for good for those who love God.

How many times do we look back over the past and realize that everything worked out for the best. We wonder why we ever doubted the outcome. What we need to do is try to remember that bit of philosophy and practice that confidence in every aspect of our lives.

Generally, if everything were to go according to our wills, it would get pretty boring. We would probably create more confusion and suffering for ourselves than pleasure. But we should strive to acquire a faith that allows us to realize that all life is governed by divine order, the purpose of which is to draw us all into a consciousness of God.

14. **OVERCOME FEAR OF DEATH**

Now we're getting into some deep water. It's hard enough to even mention the subject of losing a loved one, but to comprehend our own deaths is the most difficult of all. I honestly believe that we cannot find true peace of mind in this lifetime until we resign ourselves to this inevitable event. It is not something that might occur. It will occur. It's only a question of when.

Perhaps this is why religions came about in the first place. We all need some help in dealing with that great unknown. To my knowledge, there is no one in this world to be found who knows for an absolute certainty what is going to happen to us when we die. There are hundreds of theories, but not one that can be proved beyond a shadow of a doubt. Is there going to be a heaven like the one St. John describes in the Book of Revelation? Is there a hell for the unbelievers? Or how does reincarnation sound so that our souls keep taking on new bodies?

An Indian Guru once told me that I should liken God to an ocean and a human body to a balloon filled with the water floating around on the ocean. Death occurs when the balloon is punctured, and then our souls are blended back with God.

A Buddhist Lama described it like a stream of water approaching a waterfall. When it comes to the edge, it separates into individual droplets representing a life. Upon reaching the bottom, those droplets cease to exist and become a part of the stream again.

An agnostic or atheist would probably say that nothing happens when we die except that it is the end of our existence for all eternity.

I'm convinced that our beliefs about death drastically affect the manner in which we live. It is essential to a happy life not to fear death. We need to develop a faith that gives us the assurance that God will take care of us when we die. This is the reason that it has to be with a "childlike faith" because no one is going to be able to give us a reasonable and rational explanation that can be proved.

We may ask, "Why is it necessary to fake myself into believing something that may not be true?" To be downright pragmatic, if we can believe it, we will have a much happier life. But like C. S. Lewis said, if we don't believe and it turns out to be true, then we've lost it all. I realize that it is a dilemma for a lot of people. They can't really believe what cannot be seen, touched, smelled, or proved in black and white. I say, relax this rigid attitude, let go, and give it a try.

15. **BE FLEXIBLE.**

Each morning we make our plans for the day's activities. Sometimes everything goes according to schedule, but many times it does not. I have seen people who just get all bent out of shape if something unexpected happens. There are those who will plan their vacation to travel in a foreign country. They want to know months before they go exactly where they are going to be each and every day and what hotel they will be sleeping in each night, and some even want to know the restaurants where they will eat. "Leave nothing to chance" is their motto.

In other words, make sure that there is no adventure in the trip or as Holiday Inn advertises, "No surprises." I seem to view that as being very insecure. The true spice of life comes about many times unplanned. The most memorable moments of a va-

cation are usually things that happened unexpect-
edly. We obviously don't have much faith if we feel
that it is necessary to plan every moment of our lives.
As I have said, every once in a while, we ought to just
resign and let divine order take over. The only real
decision that we have to make is not whether we are
going to go this way or that way, but only how we react
to the events that happen in our lives. Do we act angry,
rebellious, and sullen, or do we accept divine order with
true humility, understanding, and love?

I advocate sitting "loose in the saddle." It's not
necessary to be so tight and tense about ourselves
and our lives. If something happens that throws us
for a loop, we need to learn to pick ourselves up,
dust ourselves off, and go on about our business. I
believe that things happen for a reason. We don't
always know what that reason is when it happens,
but just trust that there is a lesson to be learned in
every event that takes place in our lives as well as
the lives of our loved ones.

It is important to become more sincere and less
serious. The more lighthearted and joyful we are, the
closer we come to God. Being too serious enlarges the
ego and causes us to become more closed up. Some
people feel that if they let go, it will make them more
vulnerable. I say it is not bad to be vulnerable. In every
activity that I know in life, from playing sports to making a speech, it can be done better if we are loose and
not uptight. And that same principle applies to life.

I love the following letter written by Nadine Stair,
an 85-year-old woman from Louisville, Kentucky,
entitled *If I Had My Life To Live Over*:

"I'd like to make more mistakes next time. I'd
relax. I would limber up. I would be sillier than I have

been this trip. I would take fewer things seriously. I would take more chances. I would climb more mountains and swim more rivers. I would eat more ice cream and less beans. I would perhaps have more actual troubles, but I'd have fewer imaginary ones.

"You see, I'm one of those people who live sensibly and sanely hour after hour, day after day. Oh, I've had my moments, and if I had it to do over again, I'd have more of them. In fact, I'd try to have nothing else. Just moments, one after another, instead of living so many years ahead of each day. I've been one of those persons who never goes anywhere without a thermometer, a hot water bottle, a raincoat, and a parachute. If I had to do it again, I would travel lighter than I have. If I had my life to live over, I would start barefoot earlier in the spring and stay that way later in the fall. I would go to more dances. I would ride more merry-go-rounds. I would pick more daisies."

16. **LOVE**

And now last, but certainly not least, we come to the most important thing of all, and that is to learn how to *LOVE*.

I'm convinced that we are all crammed full of it, and most people are so frustrated because they don't have an outlet for it. This is one of those paradoxes of life, the more love we give out, the more we get back in return.

In counseling sick marriages, I've seen many couples carry around all of their frustration on their faces. They need so terribly bad to find an object to be the recipient of their affections. But they wouldn't be caught dead giving it to their spouses. He or she

is not worthy to receive it, or doesn't want it, or
doesn't know how to give it back, or ten dozen other
excuses. They either seek another person outside
the marriage or become workaholics and/or become
extremely unhappy and frustrated.

I can tell you for a certainty that it is extremely
unhealthy not to rid that love from our systems. If we
don't, it's like being bilious; we will turn green. If
we'll start letting that unconditional love flow out to
others, then it is constantly replenished. It is like
unclogging a drain pipe. Everything just starts flowing so smoothly. The more we give out, the more we
get back. And it feels so good. This is the whole
essence of our being, the reason for our existence.

Love is such a powerful thing. It can make bad
things good and change wrong to right. We should
always try to keep that drain pipe open and let that
love continue to flow out of our bodies. It is expressed in a smile, a nod, a greeting, a phone call, a
letter, a hug, and so many various ways.

I have had many Europeans tell me that the
English word for love has lost its meaning because
we overuse it. They say that their word for love is
saved and used only when it has special significance. But we say: I love hot dogs, I love the beach, I
love that car, I love hot weather, I love those sunglasses, and worst of all, we say "making love" for
having sex, when very often love may have nothing to
do with it. We have debased the word and corrupted
it. But the love that I'm speaking of is true love, the
kind that St. Paul writes about in the 13th Chapter
of First Corinthians:

"If I speak in the tongues of men and of angels, but
have not love, I am a noisy gong or a clanging cymbal.

"And if I have prophetic powers, and understand all mysteries and all knowledge, and if I have all faith, so as to remove mountains, but have not love, I am nothing.

"If I give away all I have, and if I deliver my body to be burned, but have not love, I gain nothing.

"Love is patient and kind; love is not jealous or boastful; it is not arrogant or rude.

"Love does not insist on its own way; it is not irritable or resentful; it does not rejoice at wrong, but rejoices in the right.

"Love bears all things, believes all things, hopes all things, endures all things.

"Love never ends; as for prophecies, they will pass away; as for tongues, they will cease; as for knowledge, it will pass away.

"For our knowledge is imperfect and our prophecy is imperfect, but when the perfect comes, the imperfect will pass away.

"When I was a child, I spoke like a child, I thought like a child, I reasoned like a child; when I became a man, I gave up childish ways.

"For now we see in a mirror dimly, but then face to face. Now I know in part; then I shall understand fully, even as I have been fully understood.

"So faith, hope, love abide, these three; but the greatest of these is love."

I don't know of any better way to define love than that. He pretty much said it all when he wrote that passage of scripture. So let it be.

Now this turned out to be a rather long letter, and I didn't intend for it to get too preachy. I'm continuing to learn everyday, myself, and believe me, there are still plenty of lessons I need to be taught. I have heard it said that we teach best what we most need to learn. So you can take these thoughts for what they're worth.

If for some reason the good Lord finds it necessary to take me on to the promised land anytime soon, then I would like for your boys to know my feelings about these subjects. They have been learned by a lot of painstaking trial and error. Perhaps some of my words might give them added strength to help them along in discovering life's trails.

Love,

Pops

INDEX

ABOUT THE AUTHOR

Tom Dennard was born in Pineview, a small farming community in the heart of Georgia, just like five generations of his ancestors. After attending Davidson College in North Carolina and the University of Georgia Law School, he began a law practice in the coastal town of Brunswick, Georgia. After meeting Marie Burton of Toccoa at the University of Georgia, they married upon graduation. Their three children are Susan, Ted, and Jeff. Marie owns and operates a travel agency near their home on St. Simons Island. Other than writing, Tom specializes in wills and estates for his law firm and after hours hangs out at his youth hostel south of Brunswick. His favorite hobby is mountain hiking followed by canoeing, cycling, and traveling to remote parts of the world.

Tom would welcome readers' comments:
P.O. Box 1496
Brunswick, Georgia 31521